EDGAR LEE MASTERS:

The Spoon River Poet
and his Critics

by
JOHN T. FLANAGAN, 1906 –

The Scarecrow Press, Inc.
Metuchen, N.J.   1974

Library of Congress Cataloging in Publication Data

Flanagan, John Theodore, 1906-
    Edgar Lee Masters: the Spoon River poet and his
critics, by John T. Flanagan. ⓔ

    Includes index. bibliography.
     ⓢ 1. Masters, Edgar Lee, 1869-1950--Criticism and
interpretation--History. I. Title.
PS3525.A83Z66   811'.5'2   74-20530
ISBN 0-8108-0741-6

see slip

PREFACE

This book is not intended to be a biography of Edgar Lee Masters, although such a work is definitely needed. Nor is it an exegesis of his writing and certainly not a final evaluation of his place in American literary history even if some of the responses to his many books seem clearly prophetic. Rather it is a survey of the critical reception of his poetry and prose as countless reviewers, essayists, and literary historians viewed his writing. In general I have ignored notices in the daily press unless they seemed of special significance, but I have tried not to neglect reviews in the more influential literary media both in the United States and abroad and I hope I have not overlooked the verdicts of the most important contemporaries of Masters, favorable or unfavorable as they may be.

Masters's books elicited an astonishing amount of comment from the major reviewers and critics of his day: Conrad Aiken and Amy Lowell, Carl Van Doren and William Rose Benét, H. W. Boynton and Percy H. Boynton, Floyd Dell and Ludwig Lewisohn, Bernard DeVoto and Louis Untermeyer. The phenomenon of Spoon River Anthology created a literary storm without precedent in American culture and of course produced the lion's share of comment about Masters. It is safe to say that no literary critic in the first four decades of this century could afford to be unaware of this volume of poetic epitaphy.

But many of Masters's other books also enjoyed the limelight, if less briefly. Most readers in the second half of the twentieth century will not remember that Masters was a narrative poet, a novelist, and a biographer, nor that his lives of Lincoln, Whitman, Twain, and Vachel Lindsay kept his name in the forefront of literary controversy for many years. I have thought it desirable, therefore, to record here in some detail the critical response to the books which poured forth from Edgar Lee Masters's versatile and tireless pen for almost half a century and to use basically a chronological approach. The reviews tell us a good deal not only about Masters himself but also about the literary climate of our country during the years preceding World War II.

Chisago City,
Minnesota
August 15, 1974

John T. Flanagan

TABLE OF CONTENTS

v

INTRODUCTION

When the United States Post Office released a six-cent stamp in 1970 honoring Edgar Lee Masters as an important American poet, it is likely that many of the purchasers could not identify the man thus commemorated. For even though he died as recently as 1950 his fame was already largely behind him, and the world in which he grew up and which he chronicled bore little resemblance to the world of the middle of the twentieth century. Even the small Middle Western towns which he knew so well and about which he sometimes wrote so caustically had undergone a fundamental change. Winesburg and Gopher Prairie and particularly Spoon River still existed, to be sure, but they were larger and more prosperous, perhaps even less hostile to the artist and the rebel than Sherwood Anderson and Sinclair Lewis and Masters himself had once proclaimed them to be. Moreover, the tone and trend of American poetry had changed remarkably. The analytical style which William Lyon Phelps once observed and praised in an examination of Masters's poetry was no longer in favor, earlier poetic conventions had all but disappeared, and erudition and symbolism often muddied the meaning while at the same time providing a questionable profundity for the language. The clarity, the flat forthrightness, the psychological probing which distinguished much of Masters's writing no longer characterized modern American poetry, and the man who produced a book of verse once almost as well known as Whitman's <u>Leaves of Grass</u> had gradually grown almost obscure.

But it had not always been so. For one thing Masters was an amazingly prolific writer, limiting himself not only to verse but producing book after book of biography, history, and fiction. Some fifty volumes came from his pen between 1898 and 1942 when illness closed his career. From 1914, when he finally admitted the authorship of the Spoon River epitaphs which had been appearing pseudonymously in William Marion Reedy's St. Louis Mirror, until the 1930's he was a familiar name in the American literary world, a frequent contributor of occasional verse to the magazines and the author of a stream of volumes of narrative and lyric poetry. If not exactly a leader of the literary avant-garde, he was nevertheless a conspicuous and controversial writer.

Finally, however, the critics' complaints that he had been imitating himself and continuing to write verse when he had relatively little to say began to affect his audience. Sales of his books dropped off and his style of living necessarily became modest and circumscribed. Before ill-health compelled his removal to convalescent homes he resided quietly at the Hotel Chelsea in New York City, going occasionally to meet old friends at the Players Club, lunching or dining in small restaurants near the hotel, writing a little daily but gradually taking in sail. The habit of composition remained with him, as it did with Carl Sandburg, long after silence would have been discreet. Rumor had it that old age found him practically indigent, but although the rumor was false Masters undoubtedly appreciated the award of $5,000 which the Academy of American Poets granted him in 1946. The grant at least took up some of the financial slack resulting from decreasing royalties.

When Masters died he was buried at Petersburg, Illinois, in the Sangamon Valley, the small town which had shaped his earliest views of humanity and which provided some of the characters whose epitaphs he eventually wrote. Perhaps it is appropriate that his grave is not far from that of Anne Rutledge, the girl whom he had once romanticized as the devoted fiancee of Abraham Lincoln. For his portrait of her together with his portraits of William H. Herndon and his grandmother Lucinda Matlock (Masters) prove that he could celebrate the ideal, the visionary, and the triumphant spirit as well as the failures and victims whose short and simple annals had once brought him fame.

CHAPTER 1

LIFE

In the public sense Edgar Lee Masters lived an un-
eventful life. Unlike his father he never ran for or held
political office. His legal work brought him no spectacular
courtroom fame, he traveled relatively little, and he generally avoided the lecture platform and the public forum.
He seldom addressed college audiences and never served as
a writer in residence. Perhaps these facts explain why he
has never had a full-length biography. Even when he practiced law in Chicago as a partner of Clarence Darrow his
life was largely in his books. Literary amibition drove him
fiercely. He predicted that literary success would jeopardize
his law practice and he was right in his prophecy. Prospective clients veered away from him in fear that they
might eventually join the Spoon River gallery and acquire
unwanted notoriety. But his personal life, his family, his
loves, his friendships, his reading provided ample material
for his work.

A biographer who wished to search the voluminous
papers deposited at Princeton University and the University
of Texas could no doubt fill in many of the blanks in the
biographical story, provide the dates which Masters often
forgot to insert, and identify the women whom Masters carefully failed to name. But he would have trouble giving a
better psychological picture of Masters than the poet himself
gave in Across Spoon River, the autobiography which is at
once so revealing and so enigmatic. Middle Western writers
such as Sherwood Anderson, Theodore Dreiser, Carl Sandburg, and Floyd Dell have been particularly successful in
telling their own stories and in analyzing themselves; Across
Spoon River, despite its occasional evasiveness, is one of
the best of these books.

To most people Masters is an Illinois poet, one who was conspicuously successful in capturing the flavor of rural and small town life in the prairie state even though in his view this life was often cramped, ugly, and unsatisfactory. But actually Masters was born of New England and Virginian ancestry in Garnett, Kansas, on August 23, 1868.[1]

Masters frequently alluded to his own forefathers in articles and books. In his 1933 American Mercury article, "The Genesis of Spoon River," he pointed out that his famous anthology was "a thoroughly Anglo-Saxon production." He remarked that his mother's people were Putnams, Humphreys, and Dexters in New England, while his father's people first came to Virginia in the eighteenth century. By 1829 the Masters family had settled in Illinois and the poet's grandfather, Davis Masters, spent most of his life on a farm in Menard County. A fuller account of Masters's ancestry and background appears in Across Spoon River, the autobiography which he published in 1936.[2]

The most detailed investigation of the Masters family history is included in a study by Kimball Flaccus which ran serially through five issues of Vermont History in 1954 and 1955.[3] Flaccus contended that although Masters seldom visited New England he was actually half Yankee and owed such qualities as vitality and determination to his mother. Emma Jerusha Dexter was the daughter of an itinerant Methodist minister. She went west as a young girl to visit a married sister in Kansas and while there she met Hardin Masters. The couple were married in 1867 and shortly thereafter returned to Illinois where the boy was reared. But marriage was discordant and marred by constant bickering, as Masters made clear in Across Spoon River. The mother was musical and bookish, rather scornful of the casual life of the little Illinois towns, witty and often sardonic. The father was generous, hospitable, flamboyant, a lawyer by profession and a politician by choice, a liberal Democrat who managed to win election to county offices in a generally conservative Republican area. Emma Masters resented her husband's advocacy of saloons and his refusal to attend church. Hardin Masters was unsympathetic to the passion of his wife and son for literature and did not appreciate the effort to maintain a kind of specious Yankee gentility in his prairie home. It is small wonder that this family strife was reflected in the books that Edgar Lee Masters later wrote, his poetry as well as his fiction. Indeed, he once complained in Across Spoon River, perhaps in an over-indulgence of self-pity, that his parents gave him neither direction nor sympathy.

My father did not know what to do with me, and he did practically nothing for me. The precious and abounding vitality, and intellectual hunger of those years needed to be turned to a regular course of study and cultural development in some good school, or under some competent tutor. I made my own way, finding the path after many misjudgments of the directions, and after many obstacles of circumstances, of my own making, and that of my parents. As I look back at it now it seems to me that my parents did not really care for me, or have any proper interest in me.[4]

Kimball Flaccus's study is often full of extraneous material about Vermont local history, but it gives the best explanation in print of Masters's mixed ancestry.

Masters's boyhood was spent in the Sangamon Valley, notably in the towns of Petersburg and Lewistown, communities which eventually yielded to him the characters and stories which he wove into many books. His experiences with local newspapers, his introduction to classical literature, his single year at Knox College where he studied both German and Greek, his devotion to the law under paternal pressure, and his final departure for Chicago again provided the material for much of his subsequent writing.

The young law student had difficulty in finding employment in the Chicago of 1892 but menial jobs provided subsistence for him as he learned to know the city. As a collector for the Edison Company at fifty dollars a month he became familiar with rooming houses, taverns, bars, arenas, and brothels. He met newspapermen like Ernest McGaffey and Opie Read and frequented the press watering spots. He even contributed verse under pseudonyms to the Chicago Inter Ocean and to Eugene Field's column "Sharps and Flats" in the Chicago Daily News, although he never happened to meet Field. One of his first intimates in Chicago was Ernest McGaffey (whom Masters called Maltravers in his autobiography), a young poetaster who took him to the Press Club where he met journalistic celebrities like Opie Read and Stanley Waterloo.[5] Masters's activity as a writer and publisher of verse also brought him into early contact with Harriet Monroe and her colleague in the editing of Poetry: A Magazine of Verse, Alice Corbin Henderson. Miss Monroe was not only hospitable to his poetry, but when he fell seriously ill about the time of the publication of the Spoon River Anthology she did the proofreading for him. Another contributor to Poetry whom Masters met was Eunice Tietjens, who in her autobiography published some years later left a vivid characterization of him. She had particular praise for his conversation.

He had everything, history, literature, law, science, and he remembered it all. His thoughts were continually grappling with the major problems of man's existence, with the place of religion, with historical perspective, with social adjustments. I used to hold my breath in order not to disturb him. He suffered too greatly from the only real case of world-sorrow I have ever met. [6]

A 1934 American Mercury article, which he called "Introduction to Chicago," gives specific details about his early years in the Windy City and anticipates the somewhat more discursive account he included in his autobiography. [7] He revealed here that it was through McGaffey that he met a young lawyer in need of a partner. The result was the formation of a firm for the practice of law on May 1, 1893. For something like a quarter of a century Masters was a Chicago lawyer, eventually winning a reputation for skillful cross-examination and for his pronounced sympathy with labor and the underdog. But more and more his chief interest centered in literary composition, and he devoted more time to writing than he could afford without neglecting his legal work. After he finally acknowledged the authorship of the Spoon River epitaphs he gave up his profession and left Chicago for New York City.

Eunice Tietjens also revealed a side of Masters which was seldom apparent in his serious writing but which was familiar to his friends: a relish for off-color material and for obscene humor. Masters, Miss Tietjens remarked, would suddenly "go into a huge Rabelaisian streak of pornography which was terribly starting at first." "This vulgarity," she insisted, was as much a part of him as anything else. Indeed, she boasted that she had once owned an impressive collection of Masters's pornography, equalled only in her experience by the Goethe collection in the museum at Weimar. Some of Masters's associates were offended by this trait, not the least of them his first wife.

Masters's first marriage, to Helen Jenkins in 1898, was terminated by divorce in 1923 after a stormy separation which was no doubt precipitated by a number of casual adulteries. The first Mrs. Masters, whom he referred to in his autobiography as the girl with the golden aura, occupied a stable place in Chicago society, but there were obvious temperamental differences between husband and wife which Masters did little to resolve. The index to Across Spoon River lists fifteen love affairs but gives only the first names of the women involved, and even these are often disguised. Tennessee Mitchell, for example, was referred to always as Deirdre. Perhaps the best account of this period of Masters's life was given by Dale Kramer in Chicago Renaissance, although he too was not always able to pierce Masters's reticence or deliberate concealment of his romantic experiences.8

Three children were born to this union; a son, Hardin, and two daughters, Marcia and Madeline. Masters subsequently married Ellen F. Coyne in 1926 and had a son, Hilary, by her. Although Masters frequently returned to Chicago and Illinois (where his parents survived until the middle 1920's) Masters made his later home in the east. From 1931 to 1944 he occupied rooms in the Hotel Chelsea at 222 W. 23rd Street, New York City, a hostelry sometimes called the Waldorf Astoria of Greenwich Village because at various times it was the residence of such figures as Eugene O'Neill, Arthur Miller, and Dylan Thomas. When ill-health and malnutrition afflicted Masters he was removed to Bellevue Hospital and later to convalescent homes. He died March 7, 1950 at Melrose Park, a suburb of Philadelphia.

Biographical details are scattered through a number of articles about Masters's literary work but his own writing, unreliable as it is about dates and places, is often the most informative.

Early in 1915 the English novelist and critic John Cowper Powys gave a lecture in New York City which was widely reported by the press. Powys announced that he had found three great poets in the United States: Edwin Arlington Robinson, Arthur Davison Ficke (a claim which would seem to invalidate Powys's reputation as a perceptive critic), and Edgar Lee Masters. Powys then proceeded to call Masters "the natural child of Walt Whitman," whom he in turn described as the only poet with "true Americanism in his bones." The New York Times immediately asked its Chicago correspondent to interview Masters and published the result in its issue of **April 4, 1915.9**

Masters was described by the reporter as an able lawyer given to defending the downtrodden, with a local reputation as a friend of the proletariat. The poet was described physically as "broad-shouldered and of athletic build. He has the earmarks of the lawyer and business man, and none of the traits or mannerisms of many who aspire to be called poets." Masters was pictured as modest and unassuming, very much wrapped up in his home and family--a statement which the autobiography would later contradict. The rest of the interview was primarily a recording by Masters himself of his life, his ancestry, his schooling, the residence in the Lincoln country where his father entered politics, the legal studies, the single year at Knox College, and finally his admission to the Illinois bar and his departure for Chicago. This interview, it should be recalled, preceded slightly the actual publication of <u>Spoon River Anthology</u> in book form, although the book was then in press since Masters had signed a contract with the Macmillan Company late the previous year. But the appearance of the epitaphs in <u>Reedy's Mirror</u>, from which they were widely quoted, had already won him considerable recognition. When <u>Spoon River Anthology</u> finally reached the bookstores it threatened to establish a long-time sales record. Certainly few books of poetry have ever had nineteen printings of the first edition.

Josephine Craven Chandler wrote the earliest substantial account of the models for Masters's characters, in an article entitled "Spoon River Country."10 Her rambling essay is fairly specific about people and places, and in the process of identifying some of the figures whom Masters sketched she described the geographical areas concerned and connected Masters's early life with them. Thus she emphasized that the poet conceived of Spoon River as both a town and a stream. Actually, two small rivers flowing on either side of the Illinois River are concerned, as well as a variety of communities in six or seven counties. She pointed out that while such hamlets as Summum, Bernadotte, Ipana, and London Mills belong to the Spoon River Valley, Chandlerville, Winchester, Atterberry, Clary's Grove, and Mason City are indigenous to the Sangamon River Valley. As a boy Masters knew them all and frequently visited them in his travels around the area.

The *American Mercury* article, "The Genesis of Spoon River," again provides numerous details about Masters's life in Menard, Mason, and Fulton counties, as well as sparse material about his life in Chicago when he was vacillating between literature and the law. Lewistown he described as "an organized microcosm" which also provided him with some of the happiest experiences in his life. It was at this time that he became an inveterate reader of poetry and made the acquaintance of Whitman, Goethe, Shelley, Swinburne, and Theocritus among many other bards. In Chicago he began to write poetic plays and met for the first time William Marion Reedy's *St. Louis Mirror*, the periodical which was to become his avenue to literary success. It was only a few years before Masters became a contributor to as well as a reader of the *Mirror*.

In later years Masters frequently paid tribute to Reedy for his advice and aid. Probably his warmest acknowledgement appears as a preface to his 1918 volume, *Toward the Gulf*.[11] He reminded Reedy that he owed his knowledge of the *Greek Anthology*, which had become so influential in his own work, to the perspicacity of the St. Louis editor, and he praised Reedy for his shrewd observation and understanding of recent American history. "You saw and lived, but in greater degree, what I have seen and lived," he wrote as part of his dedication of *Toward the Gulf* to Reedy. And he closed his tribute with his assurance that he appreciated their long friendship and continued to regard Reedy with great esteem and affectionate interest.

Some years after Reedy's death Masters wrote an article about him which he called "Literary Boss of the Middle West."[12] He summarized Reedy's life and sketched his personality, calling attention to his range of interests, the facility of his style, and the literary influence which he wielded. Although *Reedy's Mirror* was a weekly of rather small circulation it had an extraordinary impact throughout the country, entirely the result of the editor's energy and intellectual powers.

Reedy, on the other hand, not only encouraged Masters to contribute the famous epitaphs but in his issue of November 20, 1914 revealed the identity of their author, since they had appeared in the *Mirror* under the pseudonym of Webster Ford. He praised Masters highly for achieving both impersonality and universality. As he put it, "Mr. Masters makes great literature of his comprehensively various epitaphy by virtue of the impersonality of the work in which he makes so many other personalities live."13

The best account of the Masters-Reedy relationship appears in a biography of Reedy by Max Putzell.14 According to this account Masters first met the St. Louis editor around 1907, but the friendship ripened quickly and was cemented by extensive correspondence. Reedy published essays and verse by Masters in the Mirror prior to the appearance of the Spoon River epitaphs, although none of these early contributions attracted much attention. The epitaphs, on the other hand, brought the Mirror a celebrity which it had never previously enjoyed. Reedy himself commented on this interest in his issue of September 18, 1914. Later he published an enthusiastic letter from Ezra Pound and a verse tribute to Masters from Carl Sandburg. And, as Max Putzell pointed out, he continued to accept material from Masters after his identification of Webster Ford as a pseudonym, when better critical judgment would have insured a rejection.

Most of the essays dealing with Masters after the appearance of Spoon River Anthology in book form in 1915 discuss the work rather than the man and yield little biographical detail. There are, of course, "literary portraits," brief and surprisingly like the vitae on the dust jackets of books. A typical one in the Bookman was the work of Joyce Kilmer. In a rather facetious sketch Kilmer ridiculed the outlandish names that Masters had assigned his characters and claimed that the poet had a sense of humor despite the suicidal tone of so much of his work. Kilmer called Masters a Democrat but denied that he was either a single-taxer or a Socialist.15

A portrait which to some extent is also an interview forms the seventh chapter of David Karsner's Sixteen Authors to One. The author remembered meeting Masters some twenty years earlier when he was still associated with Clarence Darrow in a law firm. Among the qualities which impressed Karsner then was Masters's "enormous capacity for being silent and the amused and knowing look behind his spectacles." Masters punctuated his remarks with torrents of cigar smoke and revealed certain lawyer-like tricks such as speaking his most telling points in a whisper. Again, he showed a certain brusqueness, a certain scorn of irrelevancies. Karsner remarked that the poet's office had been for years a kind of confessor's box and that the Spoon River biographies were gaunt and bare as tombstones. In conversation Masters told his interviewer that writing was a lonely profession and that Chicago may have been a particular hell but proved to be a stimulant for his work. Masters also failed to acknowledge any single American book as having been influential in his poetry but asserted his intention to trace the streams of liberalism, conservatism, democracy, and aristocracy in his writing. Karsner filled out his chapter on Masters with a few biographical details which traced the family lineage back to the Revolutionary War veteran, Hilary Masters.16

Scattered biographical data do appear, however, in several sketches of Masters written during his Hotel Chelsea residence. In 1936 Georges Schreiber, an illustrator and collector, included Masters in a volume called Portraits and Self-Portraits.17 To accompany the drawing, Masters supplied an autobiographical summary of his life in which he surveyed his youth and his experiences in Chicago before settling down in the east. He confessed that he had always wanted a country residence but that insufficient funds had never allowed him to realize this plan beyond infrequent vacations and life for a short time on a Michigan farm. His literary work had been done mostly in large cities although the material for it came to a large extent from the Sangamon Valley. It might be interpolated here that the two classic accounts of life in a small Middle Western rural community, Winesburg, Ohio and Spoon River Anthology, were both written in Chicago. Masters told Schreiber that his roots remained in the country, so his outlook was really dual. His early novels about boys were obviously drawn from village life, whereas the Spoon River volumes were microcosms which interpreted human nature wherever it was. Masters attributed his impressive literary production to the habit of concentration which he had learned early and which enabled him to ignore ordinary distractions and work in the most unlikely places. He claimed that he had written much of Spoon River Anthology between receiving clients in his law office and answering telephone calls. A rather rigid adherence to plan also allowed him to finish his work according to his own schedule, even though long intervals occurred between books. Thus nine years elapsed between the two Spoon River volumes and an equal time between Domesday Book and its sequel, The Fate of the Jury. At the conclusion of his autobiographical statement he declared that poetry had been his passion from earliest youth and that it was closely allied to his devotion to music. As he reflected on his career he confessed that he might have made a mistake in writing prose at all; politics and law interested him, however, and naturally led him to an exposition of his views on these subjects. He even defended his highly controversial book on Lincoln, claiming that it was necessary to clear the public mind and to distinguish the things that Lincoln stood for from those he never could support. But poetry remained the only avenue by which one could penetrate the veil of human life and consequently poetry was the most articulate, the profoundest art of man.

Robert Van Gelder's New York Times interview with Masters is full of specific details and reminiscences. Van Gelder reported that the poet walked slowly but erectly and that he was well dressed in a blue suit which revealed his good shoulders and trim waist. Masters's ruddy face seemed to have a combative expression but actually disguised a mild, friendly manner. In reply to questions he readily gave his opinion on a variety of matters. He did not wish to be identified with a Chicago school of letters nor with the revolt-from-the-village group. He thought that amateur contributors were eating the heart out of Harriet Monroe's Poetry magazine and that the old Chicago Press Club was the hangout of drunks and unprofessional writers of sentimental ballads. As to individual writers, Masters dismissed Sinclair Lewis as a mimic whose books would not last; Theodore Dreiser had won his admiration although he felt unable to read An American Tragedy; and Stephen Vincent Benét wrote superior folk tales but had produced in John Brown's Body a poem not worth perusal since John Brown himself ought not to have been celebrated. Masters told his interviewer that he preferred Domesday Book to Spoon River Anthology and that the original manuscript of the anthology (for which he had once been offered $5,000) had disappeared since the poems were originally written at odd hours on menu cards, scraps of papers, and the backs of letters. He also confirmed to Van Gelder that although his most profitable legal case had followed the publication of the epitaphs in 1915, his law practice had been ruined by this event.18

August Derleth called on Masters twice in 1938 and 1939 at the Hotel Chelsea, meetings which he later chronicled in Three Literary Men (1963). Masters first struck him as a professional man "gone wayward into creative art." Derleth commented: "Strength and power were in his figure and in his words; he was heavy, but not fat; his eyes were challenging; his hair, somewhat long, was almost white." During the conversation Masters became almost nostalgic, even reminiscent about his father, whose death-mask he had kept. Masters remarked: "The best years of my life were spent back there in Illinois. To say that I was in revolt against village life when I was just seeing it truthfully is being just about as silly as you can get."[19] The poet also admitted to Derleth that he sometimes amused himself by writing obscene verse, which he always attributed to an alter ego, Lute Puckett.

Probably the best picture of Masters in his declining years appears in an article written by Gertrude Claytor in connection with the gift of her collection of Masters's books and letters to Princeton University in 1952.[20] Mrs. Claytor wrote an account of her friendship with the poet and his visits to her home. She described the high-ceilinged room at the Hotel Chelsea which Masters occupied for so long--a room with a fireplace, a window looking out to a courtyard in which an ailanthus tree grew, and simple furniture such as a table, bookshelves, and a rocking chair. In 1938, Mrs. Claytor observed, Masters had dark eyes, a round and rosy face, and delicate skin; his eyes could either be keen or blank with boredom. He had exceptionally beautiful hands, which were well cared for, and he wore a fine jade ring on the left little finger. She reported that at the age of sixty-nine he walked hesitantly.

Mr. and Mrs. Claytor saw Masters frequently and entertained him at their home. His friends at the time included Percy MacKaye, Ridgely Torrence, John Hall Wheelock, and various members of the Players Club with whom he would occasionally lunch or dine. In scattered conversations Masters regretted his lack of a college education, expressed his dislike of interviews, and frankly admitted his aversion to public speaking before large crowds. In contrast, he rather liked to read aloud and did so often in a clear and distinct but low voice which Mrs. Claytor did not find monotonous. His Hotel Chelsea apartment was book-lined, with preference given to poets and philosophers: Socrates, Jefferson, Emerson, and Confucius were side by side with Shelley, Chaucer, and Shakespeare. Masters confided that he once wanted to write the life of his old friend, William Marion Reedy, but that Reedy's widow would not release the necessary papers. In Mrs. Claytor's eyes Masters defined himself as an idealist, ineluctably opposed to hypocrisy, greed, and corruption; a man who was somewhat puzzled by the enthusiasm expressed for Spoon River Anthology and somewhat hurt by the cold reception accorded to later books; a poet who seemed to prefer Domesday Book among his own writings and more than once chose "To-morrow Is My Birthday," as his favorite poem.

Masters enjoyed his years at the Hotel Chelsea. It was a convenient location, close to his club and his publishers, easily accessible to his friends, in a part of New York that he liked. But in February, 1944 a friend found him seriously ill in his apartment. The obituary in the New York Herald Tribune for March 7, 1950 summarizes well the final chapter of his life. For Masters wrote no more poetry and lived as an invalid until his death.

The New York Times of March 6, 1950 devoted two columns to Masters and gave the usual summary of his life and publications. But the writer of the obituary was enormously influenced by the fame of Spoon River Anthology, which he pointed out had reached seventy editions by 1940. The book had been vilified, parodied, attacked, but it had also been defended. Not only had Masters as a result become "one of the most talked about poets in the country's annals" and an internationally known figure, but "The work probably was the most successful venture in poetry, commercially, that literature has ever known." The Domesday Book of 1920 might well be, as some critics declared, the poet's "profoundest and richest work," but the anthology was in a class by itself.

Several university libraries possess collections of Edgar Lee Masters's books and manuscripts, one of the most important being at the University of Texas. An exhibit of the material held at Austin was presented to the public from August 23 to November 30, 1968 in honor of the centennial of the poet's birth, and two years later, the Humanities Research Center of the university published a catalogue of the exhibit, compiled by Frank K. Robinson. It was a well planned tribute.21

First editions of all of Masters's books (including three borrowed from other institutions, since the Texas collection is incomplete) formed the basis of the display. In addition to these volumes there were variant editions of Spoon River Anthology, translations, galley proofs and typescripts of several books, and carbon copies of some of the verse. Manuscript material included some unpublished work, such as a short story which was reputedly a source of Domesday Book and a verse play about the Mormons entitled "Moroni." Letters from Masters to various correspondents were included, plus letters to Masters from Theodore Dreiser, Stephen Vincent Benét, Robinson Jeffers, and William Marion Reedy. Among the unliterary items in the exhibit were Masters's second typewriter, a bronze death mask of his father created by the sculptor Joseph Nicolosi at Masters's request, a medal bestowed on Masters by the Poetry Society of America, and a number of photographs--of the grandmother Lucinda Masters taken by the poet himself in 1901, of Petersburg, Illinois, with Hardin W. Masters's second-floor law office identified, and of various title pages. Pictures of Masters complete the collection. One of the last items listed in the catalogue is a novel entitled The Common Pasture, the work of Hilary Masters, the poet's son by his second marriage.

In 1972 Hardin W. Masters published a centennial tribute to his father; the brief foreword includes a number of biographical details about Masters's Chicago life--his physical stamina and his addiction to both walking and swimming, his eagerness to achieve financial independence so that he could spend his time in writing, his omnivorous reading, and his sense of humor which was evident in the letters to his friends which he signed with pseudonyms. Hardin Masters professed his own inability to judge poetry on any basis. But he devoted most of his little volume to a reprinting of a number of Masters's poems--twenty-one from Spoon River Anthology, including "The Hill"; and a handful of early poems, four from A Book of Verses and seven from Songs & Sonnets. One previously unpublished poem is also included, "The Lotus in Illinois," dated July 29, 1941 at the Hotel Chelsea. It describes the lotus in China aeons ago and the lotus along the rivers of Illinois. The poet predicted that the flower would never cease to bloom, just as the crows would always fly over Starved Rock and the hills of Bernadotte.22

Notes

1. There is some confusion about the date of Masters's birth. Various biographical dictionaries and anthologies give the birth year as 1869, a year which Masters himself confirmed at least once. But the plaque on the wall of the house in which Masters was born

in Garnett, Kansas, gives 1868; and a letter from Frank K. Robinson of May 9, 1973 to John T. Flanagan cites convincing evidence. The birth year of 1868 will be used in this study.

2. Edgar Lee Masters, "The Genesis of Spoon River," American Mercury (January, 1933), 27: 38-55; Across Spoon River (New York, 1936). Hereafter the initials ELM will be used for anything by Masters.

3. Kimball Flaccus, "The Vermont Background of Edgar Lee Masters," Vermont History (January-October, 1954; January, 1955), 22: 3-9, 92-98, 172-178, 254-263; 23: 16-24.

4. Across Spoon River, 86.

5. Max Putzell, "Masters's 'Maltravers': Ernest McGaffey," American Literature (January, 1960), 31: 491-493.

6. Eunice Tietjens, The World at My Shoulder (New York, 1938), 45.

7. ELM, "Introduction to Chicago," American Mercury (January, 1934), 31: 49-59.

8. Dale Kramer, Chicago Renaissance (New York, 1966), 173-182, 318-323.

9. New York Times Magazine Section, April 4, 1915, Section 5, 7-9. The article included a picture showing Masters wearing glasses.

10. Josephine Craven Chandler, "The Spoon River Country," Journal of the Illinois State Historical Society (October, 1921-January, 1922), 14: 249-329.

11. ELM, Toward the Gulf (New York, 1918).

12. ELM, "Literary Boss of the Middle West," American Mercury (April, 1935), 34: 450-455.

13. William Marion Reedy, "The Writer of Spoon River," Reedy's Mirror (November 20, 1914), 23: 1-2, No. 39.

14. Max Putzell, The Man in the Mirror (Cambridge, 1963).

Life

Chapter xvii, pp. 193-216, is entitled "Crossing Spoon River."

15. Joyce Kilmer, "Edgar Lee Masters, the Spoon River Anthologist," Bookman (November, 1916), 44: 264-265.

16. David Karsner, Sixteen Authors to One (New York, 1928), 125-142. Portrait drawing by Esther M. Mattsson.

17. Georges Schreiber, Portraits and Self-Portraits (Boston, 1936), 91-94.

18. Robert Van Gelder, "An Interview with Mr. Edgar Lee Masters," New York Times Book Review (February 15, 1942), 2, 28.

19. August Derleth, Three Literary Men (New York and Copenhagen, 1963), 39, 42.

20. Gertrude Claytor, "Edgar Lee Masters in the Chelsea Years," Princeton University Library Chronicle (Autumn, 1952), 14: 1-29, No. 1.

21. Frank K. Robinson, Edgar Lee Masters, An Exhibition in Commemoration of the Centenary of His Birth (Austin, 1970), 68 pp.

22. Hardin W. Masters, Edgar Lee Masters, a Centenary Memoir-Anthology (South Brunswick and New York, 1972), 62 pp. This memoir is one of a series published by the Poetry Society of America.

CHAPTER 2

EARLY VERSE AND DRAMA

Masters wrote verse at an early age and began to contribute poems to local newspapers while he was still in high school. At the age of sixteen he got a job as printer's devil at the <u>Lewistown News</u> where he learned to set type and received some encouragement to write. During his one year at Knox College he wrote sonnets, some of which were published in the Knox literary annual called <u>The Gale.</u> These fugitive pieces, like most apprentice work, are of small significance and have never been collected; moreover, many have escaped identification as Masters often signed them with pseudonyms. When he contributed verse to papers in such Illinois towns as Bushnell and Quincy he refrained from using his real name in order to conceal his authorship from his father. This habit persisted even in Chicago, where his verse appeared in the <u>Inter Ocean</u> and the <u>Daily News.</u> The long list of pseudonyms which Masters employed included Dexter Wallace, Webster Ford, Harley Prowler, Elmer Chubb, Lute Puckett, and Lucius Atherton. Masters even dedicated his novel <u>Skeeters Kirby</u> to Elmer Chubb, whom he once identified as a teacher of elocution at Zion City and who supposedly gave lessons in philosophy, rhetoric, and correct thinking. He also had calling cards printed with the name of Rev. Elmer Chubb, D.D., President Anti-Puckett Society. Lucius Atherton he transformed into a physician who occupied Suite 1311 Plow Building and who was the inventor of Fem Virigo and the purveyor of Atherton's Burglar Proof Gland Protectors. It was not until after 1915, when Masters finally admitted that Webster Ford was only a <u>nom de plume,</u> that he began to relinquish his disguises.

Masters's first printed volume was <u>A Book of Verses,</u> which the Chicago firm of Way & Williams manufactured in

1898 but never published. In his autobiography he described the book as having been "brought out in gray boards with a white label and red lettering, a book of 207 pages printed on excellent heavy paper."[1] The publishing firm turned over the entire edition, bound and unbound, to Stone & Kimball, who likewise refused to publish it, with the result that Masters, like Henry Thoreau long before him, soon found himself in possession of a substantial library, most of which he had written himself. A Book of Verses contained some sixty-eight short poems, some of them tributes to individuals such as Sappho, Byron, Whitman, and Samuel Johnson drinking wine at the dinner table, some of them dealing with mythological subjects such as Vulcan, Psyche, and Helen of Troy. There were also poems celebrating the abstractions of the seasons always favored by young poets and addressed to Flora and Autumn and Spring, and at least one piece reflecting the poet's Illinois background, "Ballade of Salem Towne." A few of the poems were reprinted in a later Masters collection, Songs and Satires. The author sent copies of A Book of Verses to some friends and potential reviewers but it was virtually ignored. Masters would have to wait almost eighteen years before he received any substantial recognition as a poet, but the virtual silence which greeted his first book did not deter him from further composition.

Between 1902 and 1911 seven plays by Masters were printed, the first of which, Maximilian, was a poetic tragedy in blank verse and was published by Richard G. Badger in Boston. It is also the only one of the seven plays to deal with historical material, the subject of course being the ill-fated emperor of Mexico. The other six plays are written in prose and deal with the contemporary scene, one or two even reflecting events and people in Masters's own life. Maximilian attracted little attention, although it was reviewed by H. W. Boynton in the Atlantic Monthly. The reviewer was not greatly impressed since he considered the basic story worthy of being treated only as opera bouffe.[2] Boynton also accused Masters of vacillating between realism and melodrama.

The six prose plays were all published by the Rooks Press in Chicago and were stimulated by Masters's basic hope that they would prove to be successes on the stage. But none was ever produced. A play called The Trifler perhaps came closest to dramatization since Harrison Gray Fiske became interested in it and wished his wife to use it;

Mrs. Fiske, however, was unimpressed and preferred to star in Edward Sheldon's Salvation Nell. Thus Masters's dream of writing commercially successful drama was never realized.

The only critical essay to deal with these early Masters plays is the work of Lois Hartley. In her Ball State University Forum article she summarized the plots of each play and reached some rather negative conclusions.[3] Althea, printed in 1907, seemed to have a certain basic reality in the critic's mind but was married by unbelievable characters and shallow thought. The Trifler (1908), Eileen (1910), and The Locket (1910) all have relationship to events in the writer's own life; Miss Hartley indeed felt constrained to summarize the Deirdre story in Across Spoon River since the two 1910 plays seem to reflect Masters's love affair with the woman called Deirdre in the autobiography, actually the sculptress Tennessee Claflin Mitchell, who later became the second wife of Sherwood Anderson. The Leaves of the Tree (1909), set in an unidentified American city, deals rather unconvincingly with both the adventures of the nouveaux riches and with the treatment accorded workers by a railroad. Again the plot seems basically improbable and the characterization mediocre. The four-act play The Bread of Idleness (1911) is probably Masters's most successful attempt to treat the problems of women in the modern world. Miss Hartley felt that in the last of his early plays Masters showed some skill in handling both character and dialogue.

Her strictures, however, apply almost equally to all the plays. The reader fails to get a clear impression of incident or characters, even though the stories have some appeal as narrative. Although Masters was hardly a trained dramatist, he had attended the theater in Chicago and he had read the Elizabethans. He understood the mechanics of a play, the need for suspense, the preparation for action, the planning of exits and entrances. Possibly his greatest fault, particularly observable in his later dramatic poems, was his inability to write dialogue which seemed both natural and appropriate to his characters.

Even in later years Masters never quite gave up the hope that he might some day write something suitable for theatrical presentation. The manuscript collection at the University of Texas contains a good many unpublished plays, one on a Mormon theme and one dealing with the story of Benedict Arnold, a subject which he had attempted as early as the 1890's.[4] And the long dramatic poems such as Richmond and Jack Kelso suggest the perennial appeal of the stage.

In 1910 Masters published his second collection of poems, Songs and Sonnets. Some of the poems were reprinted from the 1898 collection, others were new. The forty-three pieces were again a miscellany revealing no clear pattern. There were romantic lyrics, descriptive nature poetry, one or two tributes to older bards like Blake, a sequence of poems dealing with the dramatic relationship of Abelard and Heloise, and a final group of twenty-eight undistinguished sonnets. In one of the few reviews accorded the volume, William Morton Payne, the poetry critic for the Dial, called attention to the somewhat conventional structure of such a poem as "Separation" with its use of the roundel form, and noted without much approval the archaic language used by the reputed author, Webster Ford. But he also said that the "plaintive strain of Mr. Ford's decorous but deeply-felt verse is very moving, and his graceful measures have a charm that is genuine and compelling."[5]

Clearly, Masters got little encouragement from the critics who reviewed his work prior to 1915. He was simply one of a number of writers who chose verse rather than prose and who revealed metrical control and a poetic vocabulary rather than anything strikingly original or different. But on May 29, 1914 the first Spoon River portraits began to appear in Reedy's Mirror. When the anthology appeared the next year in book form, Masters was suddenly a name to conjure with.

Notes

1. ELM, Across Spoon River, 251.

2. H. W. Boynton, "Books New and Old," Atlantic Monthly, (July, 1903), 92: 124.

3. Lois Hartley, "The Early Plays of Edgar Lee Masters," Ball State University Forum (Spring, 1966), 7: 26-38.

4. Kee Robinson, "The Edgar Lee Masters Collection: Sixty Years of Literary History," Library Chronicle of the University of Texas (Spring, 1968), 8: 42-49.

5. William Morton Payne, "Recent Poetry," Dial (March 1, 1911), 50: 162-167.

CHAPTER 3

AN ANTHOLOGY IS BORN

When Edgar Lee Masters began to contribute his Spoon River epitaphs to Reedy's Mirror in the spring of 1914, he was an obscure poet who had been publishing verse for some thirty years but who had never received substantial recognition. The publication of the Spoon River Anthology in 1915 catapulted him into fame and began a critical discussion of his poetry which raged unabated for several decades. In 1924 Masters published The New Spoon River, admittedly an inferior work which nevertheless added over three hundred individual portraits to his gallery and included occupational types like the miller, barber, cobbler, tailor, and garage mechanic which previously had been omitted. These books had an impact on American poets comparable to nothing since the appearance of Whitman's Leaves of Grass.

The immediate critical reaction was varied but vigorous. Readers were undecided how to interpret the anthology: it was perhaps a portrait gallery in the tradition of the seventeenth century characters; it was a series of intertwined short stories in verse; it was a sequence of remarkably compressed verse narratives, a novel in quasi-poetic form, possibly even an epic. But the consensus was that Masters had done something genuinely creative, something which even at its inception would prove to be surprisingly influential. Cesare Pavese, considering twentieth century American literature from the vantage point of Italy, felt that no significant American writer of the period between the two world wars failed to owe something of his message and his world to Edgar Lee Masters.[1] John Cowper Powys termed the anthology the "most original work--with the exception of Theodore Dreiser's novels--that American genius had produced since the death of Henry James."[2]

21

Masters became almost immediately a towering figure in the new American poetry. Critics entitled their articles in various periodicals Masters and Frost, Masters and Robinson, Masters and Sandburg. Even ten years after the first portraits had appeared Percy H. Boynton called the anthology "the most read and most talked-of volume of poetry that had ever been written in America."3 Magazines clamored for permission to reprint some of the epitaphs or badgered Masters to contribute new ones. Through Hamlin Garland Collier's Weekly attempted to persuade him to write weekly prose portraits for its columns. The anthology even began to have an impact abroad. The London Bookman reviewed it favorably. Complete translations were eventually made into German, Swedish, Danish, Norwegian, Italian, and Dutch; partial translations appeared in Arabic, French, Chinese, and Japanese. In Italy Mario Pergallo made an opera out of Spoon River Anthology which was entitled "La Collina" and which was performed in 1950 in both Vienna and Venice. Thirteen years later Joseph Cates produced a program of readings from the Masters book called simply "Spoon River" at the Booth Theater in New York City. Some seventy of the epitaphs, interspersed with lyrics by Charles Aidman and music by Naomi Hershhorn, were read by a theatrical troupe of six. The sketches chosen for dramatic presentation included Harry Wilmans, Scholfield Huxley, Reuben Pantier, Emily Sparks, and the famous Fiddler Jones, who

ended up with a broken fiddle--
And a broken laugh, and a thousand memories,
And not a single regret.

In February, 1964 there was a London performance under the direction of David Greene. Again six actors participated and folk songs were sung by Rick Jones and Isla Cameron. George W. Bishop's review in the London Daily Telegraph of February 1 was entitled "Pithy Humour in a Graveyard." About the book itself Bishop wrote:

In form it consists of a series of some 200 epitaphs inscribed on the graves of those 'sleeping on the hill' in a country community, but in reality it presents a world in microcosm in which the inner lives and thoughts of the people are displayed with remarkable economy of language.

Ten years after the first New York performance of what was sometimes called a "dramatic revue" it was revived briefly in the same city and was enthusiastically reviewed by Peter J. Rosenwald in the Wall Street Journal for May 3, 1973. Rosenwald liked the characterizations and the performance. As he concluded,

'Spoon River Anthology' is one of those plays which takes the fabric of life, enriches it, and leaves you with a sense of understanding that makes it a must for anyone nostalgic or sentimental enough to want a fill-up of old fashioned American faith.

Masters might have been disturbed by the implication that his Spoon River Anthology, once attacked as cynical and caustic, was actually sentimental; but in any event he did not live to see his masterpiece reach the professional stage.

The vast number of reviews stimulated by the appearance of Spoon River Anthology were published in every medium of the periodical press: daily newspapers, weekly journals of opinion, news magazines, monthlies and quarterlies. They also reflected, to be sure, a wide gamut of attitudes ranging from scorn and contempt to genuine appreciation and even fulsome eulogy. Virtually every kind of critical voice was heard in these reviews: the impressionist, the literary historian, the pedant, the analytical reader, the comparatist, the literary adventurer in hot search of a masterpiece, the newspaper hack needing material for his daily stick. Given such a wide spectrum of opinions expressed in styles varying from the objective to the intemperate, it is difficult to establish any kind of pattern, particularly since the reviews ranged as much in length as they did in tone. But even the earliest notices seemed to focus on several crucial points or themes which soon became recurrent.

Critics ad initio concerned themselves with the form of Masters's book. The epitaphs were brief and concise and written of course in free verse, not in blank verse as more than one review carelessly described it. Although the anthology appeared before the free verse movement in the United States had reached its zenith, Masters certainly had predecessors in his choice of form. He was a constant reader of poetry, long familiar with the Bible, with Milton, with Whitman, and through the stimulus of his friend Reedy with the Greek Anthology. His earlier published verse had proved that he understood and could write in conventional prosody. It was probably not so much Masters's apparent brashness in his choice of form for his epitaphs as it was the ignorance of some of his critics that prompted some of the sharpest attacks on the style of his book. But since the poet eschewed rhyme and seldom used a regular metre he was severely criticized for slovenly writing.

Indeed, the basic charge from the outset was that he was not writing poetry at all but merely chopped-up prose, that he simply rearranged on the page to resemble poetry and which contained none of the other recognizable qualities of verse. Masters never used the characteristic long lines of Whitman and certainly never the sprawling, undisciplined syntax of Sandburg. But like other vers librists he employed irregular line lengths and used fewer similes and metaphors than the classical poets whose work he admired. These traits in the epitaphs often brought cries of rage from those critics who expected the regular beat of the iambic line.

A second major point at issue was the faithfulness of the depiction of the American, especially the Middle Western small town. The Spoon River Anthology preceded, if only by a few years, Zona Gale's Birth, Sinclair Lewis's Main Street, Floyd Dell's Moon Calf, Sherwood Anderson's Winesburg, Ohio and Poor White, all those volumes which in a short time would be deemed the classic documents in the fictional revolt from the village. Were the 244 characters of the Spoon River Anthology and the 321 characters of the New Spoon River Anthology actually representative of the Illinois community in which they supposedly resided? Or, to put the matter into larger perspective, did these people typify the American small town without regard to geographical boundaries in the days before improvements in roads, newspapers, radio, and television brought an end to rural isolation? Critics often asked such questions.

Certainly Masters had gone to great pains to introduce into his portrait gallery virtually all the occupations of the village. As Lois Hartley summarized his achievement,

The inhabitants include bankers, reformers, lawyers, judges, druggists, teachers, carpenters, prostitutes, poets, doctors, housewives, soldiers, day laborers, dentists, farmers, invalids, butchers, chaplains, fishermen, scientists, soldiers.[4]

Physically the list seems remarkably complete. Some had aspirations aesthetically or intellectually but met only frustrations. Masters knew no Robert Ingersoll, no William Jennings Bryan, no Stephen A. Douglas in the Petersburg and Lewistown of his youth, and none of the Spoon River people ever achieved great eminence. The villagers who comprised his generic community were people of limited capabilities, small minds, narrow horizons. But if they enjoyed few opportunities and all too often suffered from defeated hopes they were not all idlers, drones, parasites, drunkards, morons, or criminals. The weak, sinful, disreputable characters generally occupy the opening pages of the anthology; not every reader saw that Masters also drew a substantial group of admirable characters which included both martyrs and idealists. Moreover, he wrote with remarkable impersonality and objectivity. He did not flinch from presenting evil and sin but he neither condoned nor condemned. With the cold realism of the lawyer writing a brief he presented the facts as he saw them, and he allowed his faceless characters to describe themselves in these graveyard epitaphs. There is satire in the Spoon River Anthology but it is not the satire of Main Street. The people satirize themselves in their very honesty and volubility.

And there is a third point. Masters once admitted that he had entertained the notion of calling his book "Pleasant Plains Anthology," perhaps remembering that Zona Gale had once published a book about a small Wisconsin town called Friendship Village. But when the unsuitability of the title became apparent he rejected it. As a current graffito has it, "Life is a hereditary disease," and perhaps the life of Spoon River was more of a disease than life in other small communities. But Masters did not think of the anthology as a bitter, disillusioned book. Like Faulkner in later years, he was often accused of a pessimism which was actually groundless. Early reviewers were sometimes turned off by what they considered the cynicism of the portraits. Writing at a time when the genteel tradition still lingered, they reacted sharply to what they often considered to be the sordidness and even the obscenity of the epitaphs. Fred Lewis Pattee, whose taste was more catholic than most, thought that it would be intolerable to live with these frustrated, disillusioned, disappointed people. 5 And even Amy Lowell, generally hospitable to innovation and honesty, pronounced the book to be as depressing at the Newgate Calendar. To her, "Spoon River is one long chronicle of rapes, seductions, liaisons, and perversions. It is the great blot upon Mr. Masters's work."6 It must have come as a surprise to such critics to read the poet's own words in one of his best essays:

... if I had any conscious purpose in writing it and the New Spoon River it was to awaken that American vision, that love of liberty which the best men of the Republic strove to win for us, and to bequeath to time." [7]

Such a confession of intention makes it difficult to accept the charge that Masters was steeped in pessimism when he wrote his most famous work.

The most immediate reaction of magazine editors was to quote several of the epitaphs with minimal comment. Even before the anthology appeared in book form Masters's sketches were copied by various periodicals. Perhaps typical was Current Opinion, which in its issue of September, 1914 called the poems one of the most interesting experiments in semi-verse seen in some time. An editorial headnote observed that the autobiographical thumb-nail portraits were spoken by the occupants of a village cemetery and seemed to be based to a considerable degree on fact. Readers were told that the poems were written in free verse, destitute of both rhyme and rhythm but closer to poetry than to prose. Three examples were quoted: "Blind Jack," "The Circuit Judge," and "Griffy the Cooper," none of them, curiously enough, among the better known examples of Masters's gallery.[8] The October issue of Poetry paid another anonymous tribute to Masters and pointed out that the author of the epitaphs, Webster Ford, revealed something of the feeling and method of the Greek Anthology. Poetry also could find room for only three examples but it chose the prefatory poem "The Hill" and two portraits: "Ollie M'Gee" and "Doc Hill."[9] William Marion Reedy himself offered one of the best early comments in his November 14, 1914 article in which he identified Webster Ford as Edgar Lee Masters, an early contributor of other poetry to the Mirror.[10] Indeed, Reedy anticipated many of the later remarks about the Spoon River Anthology. Spoon River, he observed, was actually a composite place and was derived from communities which the poet had personally known. To his material, Reedy said, Masters brought impersonality and universality. Then, touching on the literary form of the work, Reedy remarked that it was free verse, not blank verse, and that it contained various rhythms, pure lyric notes, imagiste pictures, philosophic passages, and catalogic verses in the manner of Whitman. He admitted that occasionally Masters was so occult as to be opaque, but he insisted that the poet was a new American voice and that he wrote genuine poetry.

The year 1915 brought a number of notices and reviews. Ezra Pound perhaps blew the loudest blast of admiration in the London Egoist. "AT LAST!" he proclaimed, "At last America has discovered a poet."[11] There had been earlier poets on the western shores of the Atlantic Ocean but they had been forced to come abroad for recognition. Now, finally, "the American West has produced a poet strong enough to weather the climate, capable of dealing with life directly, without circumlocution, without resonant meaningless phrases. Ready to say what he has to say, and to shut up when he has said it." Pound referred obliquely to the earlier volume, Songs and Sonnets, only to point out that Webster Ford had improved his literary style and was no longer the "murderous derivative." Indeed, only the silly, the decrepit, the loathsome atavist would question whether the Spoon River epitaphs were poetry. Pound, too, quoted "The Hill" and "Doc Hill" to confirm his assertions.

Floyd Dell, writing in the New Republic, was rather less enthusiastic than readers familiar with his hospitality toward avant-garde literature might have expected. He did not object to Masters's use of free verse but rather to the baldness and flatness of much of the language. He felt that Masters had erred in rejecting what he called the imaginative and atmospheric use of words. On the other hand, the poet had succeeded in establishing the history of an Illinois town. "Sordid and splendid, pathetic and obscene, the life of Spoon River reveals itself."[12] Alice Corbin Henderson observed in her review in Poetry that although a sense of tragedy pervaded Spoon River Anthology it was not the kind of tragedy, hopeless and morbid and unhealthy, that appeared in much European writing. What Masters seemed to stress here was the tragedy of unnecessarily wasted lives. The reviewer also emphasized that readers ought not to miss in the book a certain flaming idealism not entirely masked by a cover of sarcastic irony. Miss Henderson quoted the portraits of Rutherford McDowell and William H. Herndon to illustrate her points.[13]

An anonymous review in the Nation was not highly specific but called attention to Masters's skill in revealing unsuspected relationships and motivations. "The history of a prairie town, its futilities, sins, aspirations, and achievements, is set forth with comprehensiveness, and with a bleak, unsympathetic species of insight." Although the reviewer wrote at a time when both novelists and poets were challenging the kind of life existing on American main streets, he objected to Masters's failure to represent the warmer and brighter side of village society. Yet he too observed in the anthology glimpses of higher goals.[14]

The notice in the Review of Reviews included a paragraph of biography and commented on the extensiveness and variety of the epitaphs.[15] The critic suggested that perhaps the book was too long and that Masters's own voice not only intruded occasionally but weakened the plausibility of the characters. But these were minor flaws; they did nothing to detract from a highly successful and unique addition to American poetry.

The New York Times Book Review printed a long, enthusiastic notice of the anthology.[16] The reviewer questioned at the outset whether any community ever existed which was so much in need of moral prophylaxis as Spoon River with its complement of drunkards, thieves, suicides, murderers, and adulterers. But the total effect, he conceded, was greater than the individual sketches. He also observed perceptively that a small village must necessarily give greater publicity to moral lapses than would a city, where vices and weaknesses could be hidden. "The village knows everything, comments upon everything, judges everything." From the immunity of the grave the Spoon River people replied to each other, gibed at hypocrisy, kept nothing back. Among the more memorable sketches were those of Archibald Higbie, the artist, and Tennessee Claflin Shope, the idealist, while lyric eloquence was particularly evident in the epitaphs of Caroline Branson and Anne Rutledge. The reviewer also considered Spoon River Anthology as poetry. He noted that the domain of verse frequently shifts or expands but that poetry and prose must have one significant difference between them: in poetry there is always a recognizable and distinct rhythm and beat. The majority of the Spoon River sketches might have been set in prose, "since the line division is arbitrary and not inherent." Yet elsewhere in the volume the rhythm is clear and of distinct beauty. The review concluded with the observation that poetry is more than form and that Masters's best sketches undoubtedly showed an art of their own.

Two important notices of Spoon River Anthology in 1915 were derogatory.[17] Raymond M. Alden in the Dial was hostile to the literary form, which he called "the reductio ad absurdum of certain of the new methods." By sacrificing conventional form Masters had not only gained nothing but had produced only questionable poetry. Alden was uncertain about the typicality of the book and claimed that some of the portraits were superfluous, yet he admitted that the anthology furnished "an extraordinary study of mortuary statistics." In only a few of the sketches could the rhythm of life be actually heard, a notable example being "Petit, the Poet." To Lawrence Gilman in the North American Review, Masters had written only "moving-picture poetry." Gilman was fully as dubious as Alden about the value of free verse. Nine-tenths of the Spoon River Anthology he called bald, flat, and uncouth, exemplified in particular by the portrait of Deacon Taylor. But he could not disguise his admiration for the originality and impact of this "village comédie humaine" nor for the poignancy of the portraits which he confessed himself unable to regard or appraise to his satisfaction. Gilman was impressed by Masters's inspired nomenclature and by his success in depicting certain character types, notably Benjamin Fraser, Minerva Jones, Mr. and Mrs. Pantier, and Frank Drummer. His label "moving-picture poetry" was explained by Masters's habit of choosing a single event which he then portrayed from several angles. The result was "a series of vivid, concentrated, rapidly shifting visualizations, related and interwoven." Gilman came to the conclusion that the book thrilled and detained the reader but its impact was not due to its merits as poetry.

Reviews and notices of the Spoon River Anthology continued to appear in great number throughout 1916. The January issue of Forum included no less than four items dealing with Masters and his anthology. Bliss Carman reviewed the book in a verse imitation of Masters's own style in which he spoke of "the spiritual sexton of Spoon River" who could be sardonically humorous and yet remain as solemn as an owl. He concluded his facetious account by remarking that the book was not one he should choose to reread and in that case it made no difference at all whether the lines were poetic or not. On the contrary, William Stanley Braithwaite found the rhythms of free verse singularly appropriate to the material and even perceived a connected story among the sketches since such a man as Thomas Rhodes figured prominently in the various events and affected other people. Braithwaite remarked that Masters revealed an unusual ability to depict characters and that his book was successful without being the typical American success or adventure story. Shaemas O Sheel denied that the anthology was a book of poems but termed it in the highest sense poetry. He also refused to use the labels novel or drama but insisted that it was substantially an epic. The anthology, to O Sheel, had clarity, variety, emotional power, and even bits of philosophy. Unlike Bliss Carman a few pages earlier, O Sheel found that the book demanded reread-ing. The most negative of the Forum critics was Willard Huntington Wright, later to become famous as the author of detective stories under the pseudonym of S. S. Van Dine. Wright found little in the Spoon River Anthology to admire. The aesthete, searching for beauty and art, might as well read a newspaper obituary. The addict of realistic fiction might better read Dreiser's novels. The philosopher would the psychologist would find Masters only superficial. Wright even denied Masters originality, contending that the poet was actually indebted for his portraiture to the earlier sketches by Edwin Arlington Robinson. It might be interpolated here that Masters categorically denied any knowledge of Robin-son's verse until well after the appearance of Spoon River Anthology. After all this derogatory comment Wright asked the rhetorical question, Why the impact, what is left? And he answered his own query by remarking that Anglo-Saxon readers relished cheap novelty, boldness of expression, and morbid sexual details, all of which exemplified "the hypo-critical Freudian reaction to a zymotic puritanism."[18]

The quartet of Forum critics certainly represented many shades of opinion about a single book and in a sense spoke for many of their contemporaries. If Braithwaite's eulogistic review was more typical, Wright's strictures were expressed with undeniable conviction and even scorn. But there were many critics who chose a more medial position.

Thus Edward Bliss Reed in the Yale Review was both critical and laudatory. He was certainly impressed by the fact that the anthology had gone through no less than eight printings in eight months, and he admitted that the idea of the book was novel. Certainly the "variety and terseness of these epitaphs attract the most careless reader and pique his curiosity."[19] But a list of dramatic personae does not make a play. Masters actually gave us only the personages and incidents for a rather sordid village chronicle. Reed also claimed that the book was exasperatingly uneven and that occasionally the characters were obviously false or trivi-al. To him the Chinaman Yee Bow was patently artificial and the volume as a whole had too many violent deaths. On the other hand, figures like Davis and Lucinda Matlock,

Isaiah Beethoven, Emily Sparks, and Aaron Hatfield impressed the reader with their vigorous reality. Reed concluded that probably Masters's greatest flaw was a lack of taste, a fault which led him to write too much. He suggested that the poet should provide an anthology of the Spoon River Anthology.

R. S. Loomis objected in the Dial to the denigration of the book since in his estimation it "faithfully mirrored a microcosm palpitant with vitality, that did not blink the worms that grope through the ordure." Loomis felt that literature should neither idealize nor fantasize. Masters did indeed deal with the trivial and often the disgusting, but he did not glorify the street walker nor the reformed drunkard.20 William Aspenwall Bradley, also writing in the Dial, called the anthology, despite its crudities, "a really notable performance." Bradley avoided the sticky issue of whether or not Masters wrote poetry by concerning himself only with larger matters. To him Masters was really not an artist at all but "a moralist and social philosopher of vague ideological tendencies."21 Joyce Kilmer, in a lighthearted "portrait" of Masters, compared him to the village atheist sitting around a New Hampshire grocery store chewing tobacco and whittling a stick while he philosophized. Even though Vermont would have been more accurate, when one considers Masters's heritage, the image is not altogether inappropriate. Kilmer then proceeded to label Masters as a Democrat who had once ardently supported Bryan and as a pacifist and progressive who had never really espoused Socialism.22

Two English reviews represent the fame of Spoon River Anthology abroad as well as the disparity of critical opinion. The New Statesman review pronounced the book a lively piece of journalistic impressionism although it welcomed signs of a new kind of poetry in the United States.23 But no reader could possibly view the anthology as a great book or even allow Masters the title of poet. "His writing is most commonplace; where he tries metaphor or any sort of high flying he is at his worst; and his moralisings, though sensible, are not profound." Three things, the reviewer thought, explained the fact that the book was easy reading: Masters's ability to profile a character in a few vivid details, his honesty of speech, and his ingenuity in using a kind of confessional for an entire community. On the other hand, C. E. Lawrence in the London Bookman was ecstatic.24 Spoon River Anthology was a remarkable piece of work, not without imperfections to be sure, but possessing reality, ingenuity, irony, insight, and vision. Blind Jack, Barney Hainsfeather, and the Village Atheist, lines from whose portraits were quoted, were among the ordinary people of Spoon River whom Masters had made extraordinary. In his verse forms Masters resembled Whitman but was more homely and less prophetic. He certainly shed no light on the mysteries beyond the tomb, but readers could hardly criticize him for not reading the riddle of life. Lawrence felt that neither recommendation nor quotation was sufficient to indicate the varied and unusual qualities of the book. It must be read and reread, and frequent perusal would be a joy and stimulus.

As World War I drew to a close and the original publication date of Spoon River Anthology receded into the background, reviewers naturally gave less space to the book itself and tried rather to assess Masters in regard to his later publications. But always the anthology remained as a kind of criterion, a bench mark, by which his subsequent work was measured. In time, of course, Masters began to resent the constant implication that he was a "one-book" man, and by continuous productivity he sought to prove both his versatility and his artistic growth. He even publicly expressed his preference for later works such as Domesday Book and various lyrics. Nevertheless, Spoon River Anthology loomed large in the background, an achievement which has remained surprisingly durable.

Two reviews which appeared in 1918 dealt nominally with a later Masters collection, Toward the Gulf, but revealed many a glance backward. Jessie B. Rittenhouse, in the Bookman, observed that the later book was generally sober and serious. "Every one of these poems is a look into the gulf, the impenetrable depth of life, and depths, as we know, are dark and forbidden." But she added immediately that Masters was the most merciless and penetrating psychologist of the day. She missed the pith and pungency of Spoon River Anthology as well as the occasional sardonic gaiety of the epitaphs. Both books, she admitted, were rather destitute of beauty, a charge which was generally made against Masters. Nevertheless, Miss Rittenhouse found something of the titan in Masters. William Lyon Phelps, writing in the same magazine, was less impressed. He commented on the poet's long apprenticeship and delayed success, and termed Spoon River Anthology a masterpiece of cynicism. Phelps found Masters most successful in his epitaphs and monologues. The longer poems such as "The Spooniad" he termed disasters. It is interesting that Phelps called "To-morrow is My Birthday," one of Masters's poorest achievements, yet this is the poem that Masters himself chose much later to represent him in a collection of the favorite poems of contemporary writers.25

Even before 1920, chapters on Masters began to appear in books devoted to American poetry in general or to carefully selected poets. Thus in 1917 Amy Lowell included a discussion of Masters and Sandburg in her Tendencies in Modern American Poetry.26 She thought that Masters resembled Strindberg more than any other writer of the age but she called Masters's work "Dostoevsky in vers libre." Among the poet's merits she cited his indomitable pluck in persevering despite lack of recognition, his genius in inventing personal names, his mastery of the succinct form of the epitaph, and his conspicuous strength, vividness, and vigor. She pointed out that Spoon River Anthology had no primary or secondary characters, no protagonist or hero in other words, but only people. What disturbed Miss Lowell in the pages of both Strindberg and Masters was their preoccupation with sex and what she considered a consequent coarseness. She claimed that Masters was more concerned with sex than any other English or American poet had ever been and, spinster that she was, she resented this. But she was quick to admit that the anthology also revealed beauty and tenderness, as exemplified by the portraits of Emily Sparks and Doc Hill. As a practitioner herself of polyphonic prose and free verse, Miss Lowell naturally expressed no aversion to Masters's poetic style; indeed she praised what she called his simple rhythms. And it should be observed that she saw at once an affiliation between Masters's poetry and the lyrics of the Greek Anthology.

A number of brief estimates followed Amy Lowell's important early critique, probably the first substantial examination of Masters's achievement by a recognized critic. In 1919 Conrad Aiken dealt with a variety of poets, including the Illinois triumvirate of Lindsay, Sandburg, and Masters, in Scepticisms.27 Aiken was unsympathetic to Lindsay's barbaric higher vaudeville and frankly scornful of Sandburg's chopped-up prose and careless rhythms. But he had sincere appreciation for Masters's Spoon River Anthology. If Masters failed as a lyric poet, he excelled as a digger-out of facts and thus did his best work as a narrator or psychological storyteller. Since Masters was by nature loquacious and discursive, his natural medium would have been prose; his choice of verse compelled him to compress. Aiken felt that Masters had strong intellectual equipment but unreliable taste and only half-accurate erudition. For this reason as well as for a tendency to write too hastily the critic expressed some doubts about Masters's chances for future survival. But he concluded that on the whole the poet's influence had been good.

Louis Untermeyer was another critic who wrote briefly about Masters in 1919. In The New Era in American Poetry Untermeyer credited the anthology with extraordinary power and originality and declared that if Masters had written only the one book "he would have remained the most arresting and vigorous figure in contemporary poetry."28 But he quickly dismissed the earlier work and found little of distinction in the works which followed. Untermeyer divided Masters's career as he then saw it into three stages: plagiarist, realist, and mysticist [sic]. He also saw a sharp break between the first and the next two. The critic's admiration for the epitaphs led him to quote extensively, and not only "The Hill" but eight portraits appear in his essay; like so many of his successors he found a kind of crescendo in "Lucinda Matlock." It was also in 1919 that Untermeyer's first edition of Modern American Poetry, a slim volume of 170 pages, appeared.29 Here he reprinted "Lucinda Matlock" and "Anne Rutledge," as well as "Silence" from Songs and Satires. In a brief footnote in the anthology he identified Masters as a resident of Chicago. Two years later, in a revised edition now including 406 pages, Untermeyer added one poem, "Petit, the Poet," but supplied a headnote in which he listed the titles of the poet's books. Untermeyer was blunt: "With Spoon River Anthology Masters arrived, and left." But he recalled the stupendous success of the volume, which was imitated, parodied, and reviled. He judged the later books to be a combination of good, bad, and derivative verse. In his general preface Untermeyer claimed that the anthology would rank as a landmark in American literature because it offered "a broad cross-section of whole communities and a great part of America in microcosm." He also pointed out that the stress on the village disillusion was not paramount since "the book ascends to buoyant exaltation and ends on a plane of victorious idealism." In later revisions of his collection Untermeyer did not substantially change his view of Masters, although it is interesting to note in the 1930 edition that he substituted "half victorious idealism" for the "victorious idealism" of 1921.30

In 1922 Percy H. Boynton contributed to the English Journal a superficial essay on Masters in which he observed that such adjectives as "queer" and "morbid" which had commonly been applied to Spoon River Anthology had also been hurled at Whitman.31 Boynton admitted the shock value and novelty of the book and asserted that such qualities had won it an unusually large audience. But he insisted that, given Whitman's frankness, Browning's analytical gifts, and Freud's bias, Masters was bound to write startling passages. Like other academic readers, Boynton was disturbed by Masters's tendency to dwell on passion and lust in his portraits.

Harry Hansen, a newspaperman who knew most of the Chicago writers who frequented Schlogl's Restaurant, dealt with a number of the literati in Midwest Portraits, a book notable for its personal insights.32 For some curious reason Hansen linked the novelist Robert Herrick and Masters in the same chapter and gave Herrick twice the space he accorded the poet. Hansen made the usual comment that Masters had published a good deal of verse, often dignified and unoriginal, before the famous epitaphs appeared, and that this early poetry hardly predicted the poet's later celebrity. But there was something of the exhorter or prophet in Masters, as well as a keen understanding of political affairs. Hansen also remarked that Masters had always been concerned with the impact of the community on individuals, a concern clearly manifested not only in the anthology but in the narrative poem, Domesday Book, and in the 1923 novel, Skeeters Kirby.

Another Chicago journalist, Llewellyn Jones, published an essay on Masters in First Impressions.33 Jones, like Amy Lowell previously, was quick to point out Masters's indebtedness to the Greek Anthology but claimed that the Spoon River poems were a criticism of life and neither strange in form nor ugly in substance. Indeed, he said of the anthology: "It is an undoubtedly veridical picture of a small town rotten because it is out of touch with the currents of modern life." Its people "either live parasitic lives on their poorer neighbors, escape, by fair means or foul, or else they die the victims of their surroundings." But he refused to admit that the book was altogether black and sordid. Portraits like that of the Village Atheist certainly exemplified Masters's strong bent toward mysticism.

The English novelist May Sinclair was rapturous about both the original anthology and its sequel.34 The New Spoon River was every whit as good as its predecessor; indeed, both volumes showed the same poignancy, the same relentless sincerity, the same hard and clear simplicity, and the same naked reality. Masters, she thought, had the ability to delineate a whole character in anything from three lines to seventy-five. To exemplify her point she quoted the portraits of Howard Snively and Sarah Dewitt from the sequel. Miss Sinclair concluded her tribute with lines that must have gratified Edgar Lee Masters. Not only did Spoon River Anthology reveal the essential genius of American poetry in a way unsurpassed since Walt Whitman, but she could not conceive of the Spoon River poems being forgotten: "as long as the English-speaking races live they must endure."

In 1924 John Farrar edited The Literary Spotlight, a series of sketches of prominent American writers of the period accompanied by caricatures by William Gropper.35 The sketches were anonymous and generally dealt more with the personalities and reputations of their subjects than with critical evaluation of the work. Thus the essay on Masters included the following jeu d'esprit from the pen of Keith Preston of the Chicago Daily News:

Gaudeamus Igitur

Edgar Lee Masters doesn't like Chi;
Furthermore he tells us the why!
Firstly he thinks we are drying as drinkers:
Second he thinks we are trying as thinkers.
Edgar Lee Masters doesn't like Chi.
What'll we do? Lie down and die?

Never, no, never! Edgar would laugh,
Write us a helluvan epitaph.
Read the Anthology, brothers, and shiver!
Shall we be dumb as the dead of Spoon River?
Lo, these poor hicks that lay under the asters!
Living at least we annoy Mr. Masters.

The author of the essay, however, stressed the fact that Masters was a kind of solitary who separated himself from the literary and intellectual life of Chicago. As a lawyer Master had been capable and aggressive, particularly adept at cross-examination. He was also known for his interest in humanitarian causes, although he often sacrificed his professional life to devote more time to his writing. There could be no doubt about the success of Spoon River Anthology but subsequent books tended to be medleys. As the critic put it, "There are poems, romantic and biblical, tirades, catalogues, and psychopathic sketches." But Masters did have a streak of sardonic humor which readers often overlooked. He once contributed a series of sonnets to Reedy's Mirror under the name of Elmer Chubb which were fulsome hoaxes, like nothing so much as "the savage twinkle of a rogue elephant."

More serious estimates came from the pens of Clement Wood and Harriet Monroe. Wood, in Poets of America, took a decidedly negative position. He did not object to Masters's stress on sex and violent deaths but rather to his lack of skill.36 Inept rhetoric and awkward stylistic inversion were sufficient proof of the poet's lack of artistry. Wood, in fact, thought that Masters was the poorest of any of the current practitioners of verse who enjoyed a substantial reputation. Spoon River Anthology, to be sure, had attained great popularity but not on the basis of its poetic merit. Rather, it was the narrative quality, the sharp human portraits such as those of Lucinda Matlock, Enoch Dunlap and Editor Whedon that explained the surprising public appeal. Wood expressed his final estimate of the anthology in a kind of epigram: the book was more antidote than art.

Harriet Monroe, perhaps remembering that she had been hospitable to Masters in the columns of Poetry, wrote more cautiously and gave measured praise.37 She thought that Spoon River Anthology illustrated an old principle: present a local group completely and honestly and you will present the race. Masters had successfully depicted Illinois, the heart of Middle Western America, but Lucretius and Li Po and Omar would have recognized the types and incidents. The terse little epitaphs fitted their material perfectly and gave to the book a kind of epic stature. Like some other friendly evaluators Miss Monroe saw in Masters both a sense of humor and what she called a "splendid burning candleflare of beauty," especially in the portraits of Anne Rutledge and Lucinda Matlock. She was also kinder than most reviewers in her estimate of some of the poetry that succeeded Spoon River Anthology. In her review of the sequel she approved of the supplementary biographies and found no repetition there.38 The poet's "capacity for fierce living and hard thinking is what gives size and depth" to his work.

She pointed out that to Masters the unpardonable sin was the desecration of human life, and she commended him for making full use of American epic material. But she could not avoid a final wry note: she believed that a more systematic and dramatic arrangement would have eliminated one-fourth of the epitaphs.

The appearance of The New Spoon River, nine years after the original anthology had been published, evoked a few reviews in which the writers attempted a comparative approach, although a close analysis of the two books remained for later critics to achieve. Carl Van Doren in the Century was sparingly laudatory.39 He observed that some changes had taken place in Spoon River, which was now a suburb of Chicago. Some changes had also taken place in Masters. The poet was now less inclined to let his characters speak for themselves, with the result that the book was repetitious and had something of the polemic about it. Nevertheless, Masters had enlarged the graveyard and the additional stones still spoke eloquently. Van Doren felt that Masters had not produced poems of special eminence and he mentioned no characters by name. O. W. Firkins wrote a careful analysis for the Saturday Review of Literature which is notable for its clarity and precision of statement.40 He commented that the Spoon River method was congenial to Masters's faculty but uncongenial to his temper. The terseness of the epitaphs was still remarkable but fewer of them were basically biographies. Firkins thought that Masters had devoted too much time to argument and discussion; moreover, many of the characters were simply proxies for their creator, a fact which did not make for drama. Firkins anticipated later critics in pointing out similarities between Masters and Browning, especially in their fondness for dramatic monologue and in their tendency toward the speculative. In The New Spoon River the gravestones have settled a bit and the grass has thickened. But Masters touched on many current issues and expressed clear thought in a small compass. Firkins, at the end of his review, touched on the occasional lyric qualities of the book and commended Masters especially for the portrait of Howard Lamson. He called the final line nobly imaginative: "My dream is what the hill-side dreams."

The attitude of the establishment of the 1920's toward Masters is well represented by the tirade of Henry Van Dyke, whose bland conventionality once made him a popular writer. In his essay "A Dark Lantern" Van Dyke denied

Masters any claim to novelty and originality: he had been preceded by Whitman, Crabbe, and Charles Lamb. Spoon River must have been a horrible place, he argued, if Masters as necrologist could be relied on. Van Dyke quoted the epitaphs of Barney Hainsfeather, Homer Clapp, and Lydia Puckett, all of which he called desiccated biographies, and remarked that anyone could imitate them by forcing a short story into a hydraulic press, squeezing it hard, and putting the remainder into broken lines. Masters's so-called verse was in fact "chop-stick prose,--knock-kneed, splay-footed, St. Vitus prose." As for Masters's later verse, it was less interesting than the Spoon River portraits.[41]

Subsequent writers reiterated previous critical comments but were often inclined to take a middle-of-the-road position. Thus Bruce Weirick, in From Whitman to Sandburg in American Poetry, argued that Masters had revolted against his time in two ways: against the Puritanism evident in art, morals, and religion, and against the greed and corruption all too apparent in politics and business. If the Spoon River poems were realistic they were all too often cynical and, moreover, they gave a one-sided view of village life in the Middle West. Weirick agreed with Amy Lowell that Masters took a morbid interest in sex, which led him into needless exhibitionism. The same qualities were obvious in Domesday Book despite a quite different structural framework.[42]

Sharper criticism appeared in Alfred Kreymborg's Our Singing Strength, in which Masters was compared unfavorably with Sherwood Anderson and Carl Sandburg.[43] Kreymborg claimed that there was more poetry in Winesburg, Ohio than in Masters's verse and felt that Sandburg had a much more sensitive ear for human speech. Kreymborg did not object to Masters's free verse per se, only to its prosaic and bald quality. He paid little attention to the philosophy or even the realism of the portraits but concentrated on the inferior artistry. Masters, although an excellent storyteller and a devotee of truth, was both careless and insensitive. To summarize, Kreymborg believed that Masters simply did not know how to sing.

Kreymborg's view was echoed and indeed quoted by Fred Lewis Pattee, one of the early academic specialists in American literature.[44] Although Pattee was generally hospitable to the new voices in twentieth century literature, he was unable to perceive the singing quality of great poetry in

Spoon River Anthology. Moreover, he claimed that Masters had made little effort either to characterize or to describe his people. The epitaphs did not always tell the whole life but centered rather on a single situation, and not necessarily the most influential one. Pattee remarked that Masters's legal training often affected his writing adversely since it led him to act like a prosecutor in a criminal case and to stress only certain kinds of evidence. Both the Kreymborg and Pattee essays, written some fifteen years after Spoon River Anthology, expressed serious reservations about the permanent importance of the book.

By the third decade of the twentieth century anthologies of the so-called new poetry began to appear and Masters was given conspicuous space. In Chief Modern Poets of America, edited by Gerald D. Sanders and John N. Nelson in 1929, with a revised edition seven years later, Masters was one of fifteen poets represented and received forty-three pages. It might be interpolated here that when Roy Harvey Pearce published his Continuity of American Poetry in 1961 he squeezed Masters into two paragraphs on two different pages but allotted Wallace Stevens fifty pages. The Sanders-Nelson collection used thirteen poems from Spoon River Anthology and ten from the sequel. The four-page preface recited the main facts about Masters's personal and literary life but generally refrained from making evaluative judgments. A contemporary reader who might examine the Sanders and Nelson anthology would note immediately that Masters was given the first position, but this accolade of "primus inter pares" was purely coincidental: he was simply the oldest of the poets included.45 On the other hand, he was accorded as much space as Robinson and several times as much as that allotted to Pound or Eliot.

After 1930 the essays and articles dealing with Masters were generally not specific examinations of Spoon River Anthology but either discursive discussions of his entire work or analyses of the other literary forms that Masters employed. Only a few of the later treatments are relevant at this point.

In 1932 A. C. Ward, an English critic, commented on the Spoon River epitaphs and pointed out their lack of proportion.46 He thought they were a salutary correction to the syrupy conventionality of much of the verse current when Masters first published them, but he argued that the correction had been overdone. Masters, in his excellent work of sardonic protest and righteous indignation, had simply gone too far. Ward suggested that Spoon River Anthology itself should be anthologized and those portraits which were obviously stagey and even ludicrous should be eliminated. Ward also joined the chorus of protest against the style: the verse was "often poor and occasionally on the level of chopped prose from a small-town newspaper." Since these people pronouncing their own epitaphs would normally have been inarticulate, the poet ought to have been able to supply speech for them which possessed greater force and color.

The next year, Herbert Ellsworth Childs took a very different approach in his analysis of Masters's work. He called the poet essentially a Jeffersonian Democrat of the old order, with natural beliefs in economic determinism, the nobility of the common man, a preference for strong local government, and the need to protect the citizenry from special privilege. These beliefs, Childs argued, came out strongly in Spoon River Anthology, since the community itself represented a failure in social justice. All Masters's portraits, to him, were tarred with the brush of agrarianism, a defunct philosophy now but one which contained the seeds of liberalism. Agrarianism compelled Masters to discuss public morality; a hostility to convention stimulated him to deal with private morality and to depict individuals who were dissatisfied with monogamy as a way of life. Childs admired Masters for his candor in handling such subjects but felt that he erred in suggesting no solution. Agrarianism was no longer the answer for the problems that Masters raised, and he offered no other.[47]

In 1939 Ina Honnaker Herron devoted a long section of her chapter on "Crusaders and Skeptics," in her Small Town in American Literature, to Masters.[48] She reviewed in some detail Masters's preparation for writing the book and its organization, since she felt that the notoriety of Spoon River Anthology demanded such a reexamination. Miss Herron observed that the book possessed neither primary nor secondary characters, merely the people of a small Middle Western town. Local realism was one of its significant qualities despite the fact that Spoon River consisted of traits derived from the poet's knowledge of such actual places as Petersburg, Lewistown, New Salem, and Hanover. Thus, "The prevailing American qualities of the cramped, monotonous lives of an ugly little river town show Masters to be an observing poet of the absolute, of the real." Masters, in Miss Herron's words, revolted against the stale conventionality of small town life and was disturbed by the general de-moralization of Spoon River. She recapitulated some of the common charges levelled at the book; for example, Mas-ters's obsession with crime and sordidness and his willing-ness to chronicle seductions, liaisons, and perversions. She also alluded to the common criticism of the "Spooniad," the incomplete fragment of epic poetry supposedly written by the laureate of Spoon River, Jonathan Swift Somers, which served as an appendage to the volume. By 1939, as Miss Herron frankly observed, many critics of Spoon River Anthology had been too much influenced, even perhaps too fascinated, by the indictment of small town life in Masters's portraits to realize that it was not a completely one-sided delineation. Obviously, Masters not only acknowledged the presence of loyalty, love, and spirituality in the average small community, but presented some of his characters as the happy conquerors of circumstances. Miss Herron praised Masters for his extraordinary range of vision and called Spoon River Anthology "a masterpiece which might well be termed an epic of everyday American life." She concluded that the poet had contributed significantly to the annihilation of the sentimental idea that the American small town was the repository of virtue and happiness.

In the next three decades few articles concentrated on Spoon River Anthology, although any discussion of Masters could hardly avoid the book. The Swiss critic Heinrich Straumann, in his streamlined discussion of twentieth century American literature, could devote only a few paragraphs to Masters. Nevertheless, he termed the book an extraordinary achievement and commended it as an astonishingly complete picture of the lives of the inhabitants of a small middlewestern community. Straumann perceptively remarked that Masters's chief concern was the discrepancy between appearance and reality in human life. To interpret the enigma of existence the poet chose the psychological approach and in the process produced some of his most striking portraits. 49 In 1953 John T. Flanagan contributed to the Southwest Review a survey of Masters's poetry as a whole, and strove to find excellence in some of the later writing. But the critic had to admit that with the exception of Domesday Book the long narratives were prosy and dull, while some of the nostalgic lyrics which Masters eventually wrote about the Illinois landscape were little more than charming miniatures. 50 Invariably, the reader of Masters had to return to the anthology for satisfaction. The Spoon River characterizations had a solid base in reality, they were psychological rather than physical portraits, they were notable for their candor and acerbity, and they revealed in the closing section a strong idealism. Flanagan concluded that although Masters's fame undeniably peaked in the years following World War I, it was inconceivable that he would be reduced to a footnote in subsequent literary histories.

Two late articles compare Masters with his contemporaries. Ernest Earnest argued in the Western Humanities Review that the Spoon River poet had some similarities with Eliot even though The Waste Land changed the diction of modern poetry and alienated audiences from the earlier verse.[51] Both Masters and Eliot clearly represented society as arid and sordid and each through careful vignettes presented a panoramic view of that society. Both poets, furthermore, glamorized a somewhat mythical past at the expense of the present. Earnest noted that differences in technique were most apparent. Masters's material resided in his poetry, Eliot's outside (witness the erudite notes for which he became famous). The critic contended that the anthology was "essentially a picture of a society maimed by puritanism, materialism, narrow religion and hypocrisy." Its enormous success was due to the brevity of the sketches, their ironic view of life, and the frequently aphoristic conclusions.

Robert N. Hertz, in the Minnesota Review, restated the earlier views of critics that Masters and Robinson were much alike. He found Robinson the more romantic, Masters the more realistic. Both poets represented village life, one in Maine, one in Illinois, but Robinson's characters, generally male, lived on the periphery of the conventional social world while the Spoon River people were closer to the core of the community. Masters's characters were immediately recognizable and, although not conspicuously wicked by modern standards, did speak frankly about their trespasses. Hertz observed incidentally that although Robinson revealed his own philosophy rather clearly in his poetry, Masters was generally more reticent.[52]

In some ways the most satisfactory of the recent treatments of Spoon River Anthology is the work of the late Lois T. Hartley. Miss Hartley wrote the first doctoral dissertation to deal with the work of Masters in 1949 at the University of Illinois. Segments of her study appeared in various journals and in 1963 she produced a valuable monograph.[53] Although not basically evaluative it deals with almost all the genetic and structural aspects of the anthology and utilizes all the relevant criticism which had previously appeared. Much of Miss Hartley's material was necessarily repetitive. She summarized Masters's early experience as a poet, his persistent efforts to establish himself as a writer, his obligations to books such as the <u>Greek Anthology</u> and to friends like William Marion Reedy. When Reedy rejected some of Masters's conventional verses but accepted the Spoon River sketches, many of which reached his office pencilled on scraps of paper, Masters was well on his way to fame. Miss Hartley surveyed the geographical background of the poems and identified many of the physical models. She commented on the nomenclature of the characters and observed, like many previous critics, that the stories were often deliberately interconnected, sometimes even parallel. By 1963, of course, the order of the anthology was well understood and few readers could miss the change in tone as the misfits and failures were succeeded by the martyrs, philosophers, and idealists. Even so, the picture of the sordid, drab, disillusioned village folk remains indelible.

Miss Hartley was among the few critics to make a substantial comparison of the original <u>Spoon River Anthology</u> of 1915 with the sequel published nine years later. She observed some specific differences between the two volumes. Not only had Spoon River itself changed in the interval but new occupations were apparent among the townspeople and the inhabitants themselves were no longer so obviously Anglo-Saxon in origin. When Marx the sign painter practiced his profession he had to deal with funeral parlors, life insurance agencies, and the automat. McDowell Young observed names in Spoon River like Berkowitz and Geisler, Lukasewski and Koslowski. As Masters himself put it, the small village of Spoon River, a rural backwater, had suddenly become "a ganglion/For the master brain Chicago."[54] But the more things change, the more they remain the same. Bruno Bean the auto mechanic spoke very much to the point: "I saw no change in the game of men, And nothing gained by the swifter wheels."[55] In general, the two Spoon River books have more resemblances than dissimilarities. Each consists of autobiographical epitaphs, many of them interrelated. Instead of the opening poem entitled "The Hill" in the original collection, there is the initial poem "The Valley of Stillness" in the sequel. Some of the portraits seem to be constructed along similar lines and the same ironic humor appears in both books. As Miss Hartley put it, "He [Masters] still praised honesty, courage, magnanimity, and vitality." One comment, however, should be stressed. The New Spoon River epitaphs were certainly less concerned with sex and violent death; instead, speculative, political, and philosophical themes demanded more attention. As a result, the book suggests that Masters had become somewhat less objective. Indeed, Miss Hartley concluded that too many voices were those of Masters himself, not those of the characters, so that the personalities of the speakers became unfortunately shadowy.

In the decade of the 1960's paperback reprints of the two anthologies appeared, each furnished with a perceptive introduction. May Swenson, in her foreword to Spoon River Anthology in 1965, commented on the sexual frankness of Masters and called him the Kinsey of his day. As she wrote, "Few of the ingredients of human corruption and vulnerability are missing from the dispositions of these underground witnesses, and the Anthology remains fascinating if for nothing else than to untangle the lurid web of small town scandal provocatively placed before us."[56] Willis Barnstone, in his preface to the New Spoon River, was especially concerned with Masters's indebtedness to a classical source and pointed out that the poet had read carefully J. W. Mackail's Select Epigrams from the Greek Anthology in the 1906 edition. Barnstone contended that Masters owed much of both the mood and form of his book to the Greek original, not just the epigram but the interrelated voices. He also compared the two anthologies and made an interesting value judgment: if the original Spoon River Anthology contains more good poems, the best poems of the New Spoon River are superior to any published earlier, chiefly because they are more desperate, more violent, and more tragic. Barnstone also commended Masters for his surprising modernity in the use of colloquial speech, almost as if he were a playwright recording what he overheard on the streets.[57]

Many of the briefer estimates of Spoon River Anthology and its sequel appeared not in specific essays but in histories of American poetry or of American literature in general, surveys which began to appear with increasing frequency around the mid-century. These will be considered in the final chapter of this book.[58]

Notes

1. Cesare Pavese, "The Dead at Spoon River," _American Literature, Essays and Opinions_ (Berkeley, Los Angeles, London, 1970), 179.

2. John Cowper Powys, "Edgar Lee Masters," _Bookman_ (August, 1929), 69: 650.

3. Percy H. Boynton, _Some Contemporary Americans_ (Chicago, 1924), 52.

4. Lois Hartley, _Spoon River Revisited_, Ball State Monograph Number One (Muncie, Indiana, n. d. [1963], 7.

5. Fred Lewis Pattee, _The New American Literature 1890-1930_ (New York & London, 1930), 288.

6. Amy Lowell, _Tendencies in Modern American Poetry_ (Boston & New York, 1931), 175.

7. ELM, "The Genesis of Spoon River," _American Mercury_ (January, 1933), 27: 55.

8. "Voices of the Living Poets," _Current Opinion_ (September, 1914), 57: 204.

9. "Our Contemporaries," _Poetry: A Magazine of Verse_ (October, 1914), 5: 42-44.

10. William Marion Reedy, "The Writer of Spoon River," _Reedy's Mirror_ (November 20, 1914), 23: 1-2, No. 39.

11. Ezra Pound, "Webster Ford," _Egoist_ (January 1, 1915), 2: 11-12.

12. Floyd Dell, _New Republic_ (April 17, 1915), 2: 14-15.

13. A[lice] C[orbin] H[enderson], "Reviews," _Poetry: A Magazine of Verse_ (June, 1915), 6: 145-149.

14. _Nation_ (May 27, 1915), 100: 604.

15. _Review of Reviews_ (June, 1915), 51: 758.

16. "A Human Anthology of Spoon River," New York Times Book Review (July 18, 1915), 261.

17. Raymond M. Alden, "Recent Poetry," Dial (June 24, 1915), 59: 26-30; Lawrence Gilman, "Moving-Picture Poetry," North American Review (August, 1915), 202: 271-276.

18. All four notices appeared in the January, 1916, issue of Forum, volume 55: Willard Huntington Wright, pp. 109-113; Bliss Carman, pp. 114-117; William Stanley Braithwaite, pp. 118-120; Shaemas O Sheel, pp. 121-123.

19. Edward Bliss Reed, Yale Review (January, 1916), 5: 423-426.

20. R. S. Loomis, "In Praise of Spoon River," Dial (April 27, 1916), 60: 414-415.

21. William Aspenwall Bradley, "Four American Poets," Dial (December 14, 1916), 61: 528-530.

22. Joyce Kilmer, "Edgar Lee Masters, the Spoon River Anthologist," Bookman (November, 1916), 44: 264-265.

23. "The Transatlantic Lyre," New Statesman (January 8, 1916), 6: 332.

24. C. E. Lawrence, "Somewhere Near Helicon," London Bookman (March, 1916), 49: 187-188.

25. Jessie B. Rittenhouse, "Contemporary Poetry--News and Reviews," Bookman (April, 1918), 47: 201-203; William Lyon Phelps, "The Advance of English Poetry in the Twentieth Century," Bookman (May, 1918), 47: 255-269.

26. Amy Lowell, Tendencies in Modern American Poetry, 139-198.

27. Conrad Aiken, Scepticisms (New York, 1919), 65-75.

28. Louis Untermeyer, "Edgar Lee Masters," The New Era in American Poetry (New York, 1919), 161-181.

29. Louis Untermeyer, Modern American Poetry (New York, 1919).

30. Louis Untermeyer, revised and enlarged edition (New York, 1921), 119-121. Preface p. xxxiii. Fourth revised edition (New York, 1930). Preface pp. 17-18.

31. Percy H. Boynton, "The Voice of Chicago: Edgar Lee Masters and Carl Sandburg," English Journal (December, 1922), 11: 610-620; reprinted in Some Contemporary Americans, 50-71.

32. Harry Hansen, "Robert Herrick and Edgar Lee Masters, Interpreters of Our Modern World," Midwest Portraits (New York, 1923), 225-251.

33. Llewellyn Jones, "Edgar Lee Masters: Critic of Life," First Impressions (New York, 1925), 69-84.

34. May Sinclair, "Edgar Lee Masters Works a Miracle," Literary Digest International Book Review (December, 1924), 3: 32.

35. John Farrar, "Edgar Lee Masters," The Literary Spotlight (New York, 1924), 224-231.

36. Clement Wood, "Edgar Lee Masters: Caliban Upon Helicon," Poets of America (New York, 1925), 163-180.

37. Harriet Monroe, "Edgar Lee Masters," Poets and Their Art (New York, 1926), 46-55.

38. H[arriet] M[onroe], "Spoon River Again," Poetry: A Magazine of Verse (February, 1925), 25: 273-278.

39. C[arl] V[an] D[oren], "Hark Again from the Tomb," Century Magazine (January, 1925), 109: 430-431.

40. O. W. Firkins, "The Return to Spoon River," Saturday Review of Literature (October 11, 1924), 1: 178.

41. Henry Van Dyke, The Man Behind the Book (New York and London, 1929), 98-111.

42. Bruce Weirick, From Whitman to Sandburg in Ameri-

can Poetry (New York, 1930), 195-200.

43. Alfred Kreymborg, A History of American Poetry (New York, 1934). Originally published in 1929 as Our Singing Strength, 379-385.

44. Fred Lewis Pattee, The New American Literature 1890-1930, 285-290.

45. Gerald D. Sanders and John H. Nelson, Chief Modern Poets of America (New York, 1929), revised edition 1936.

46. A. C. Ward, American Literature 1880-1930 (New York, 1932), 166-168.

47. Herbert Ellsworth Childs, "Agrarianism and Sex, Edgar Lee Masters and the Modern Spirit," Sewanee Review (July-September, 1933), 41: 331-343.

48. Ima Honaker Herron, The Small Town in American Literature (Durham, 1939), 353-366.

49. Heinrich Straumann, American Literature in the Twentieth Century (London, 1951), 137-139.

50. John T. Flanagan, "The Spoon River Poet," Southwest Review (Summer, 1953), 38: 226-237.

51. Ernest Earnest, "Spoon River Revisited," Western Humanities Review (Winter, 1967), 21: 59-65.

52. Robert H. Hertz, "Two Voices of the American Village: Robinson and Masters," Minnesota Review (Spring, 1962), 2: 345-358.

53. Lois Hartley, Spoon River Revisited, 3-30.

54. ELM, The New Spoon River (New York, 1924), 26.

55. ELM, The New Spoon River (New York, 1968), 9.

56. May Swenson, Introduction, Spoon River Anthology (New York, 1965), 12.

57. Willis Barnstone, Introduction, The New Spoon River (New York, 1968).

58. A note about the popularity, or perhaps notoriety, of Spoon River Anthology may be in order here. In 1972 an English teacher in the Hillard Junior High School of the Scioto-Darby City School District in Ohio ordered copies of the book for a text for his ninth grade students. When the copies arrived the students discovered that, on orders of the school principal and superintendent, three of the portraits (Georgine Sand Miner, Elijah Browning, and Daniel M'Cumber) had been removed from the books, presumably because they contained objectionably explicit sexual material. See School Library Journal (January, 1973), 98: 206-207. A number of students signed a petition requesting unmutilated copies.

CHAPTER 4

SOME INTERMEDIATE COLLECTIONS

Between 1915 and 1921 Edgar Lee Masters published seven books. One was his first novel, Mitch Miller; one was his first long narrative poem, Domesday Book; and five were books of miscellaneous verse. All of them were reviewed fairly widely without conspicuous enthusiasm on the part of the reviewers. There was not, to be sure, wholesale condemnation; many a critic singled out individual poems for accolades or commended Masters for insight and skill in characterization. But the consensus seemed to be that the poet had not equalled Spoon River Anthology in achievement and had certainly not advanced beyond it either in originality or in artistry. Moreover, the flaws that reviewers noted in the first of the five books of verse to appear, Songs and Satires in 1916, became distressingly familiar to readers by the time The Open Sea was published in 1921. The complaint seemed to be not that Masters failed to justify attention and even respect but that he continued to show the lapses of bad taste and careless writing that had disturbed earlier critics. One might profitably examine the scope of the two first books to appear since they established a kind of pattern for the other three.

Songs and Satires contains some 45 miscellaneous poems. A few are in vers libre but most conform to conventional verse, rhymed lines or blank verse, stanzas in various combinations. One of the best, "Silence," which was often quoted, is in free verse. The narratives "Arabel" and "Jim and Arabel's Sister" are in undistinguished blank verse. Masters even tried his hand at the familiar ballad and used Arthurian subjects.

The arrangement of poems in the book shows no pattern whatsoever but does reveal an amazing variety of themes. At least two poems are tributes to men he admired, William Marion Reedy and William Jennings Bryan (in the poem called "The Cocked Hat"). Mythological themes appear in at least two, "The Vision" (in which the poet imagines he sees Apollo) and the very trite "Helen of Troy," an early poem which Masters indiscreetly preserved and which consistently annoyed reviewers because of its clichés. Imitation ballads like "St. Francis and Lady Clare" and "The Death of Launcelot" provide another category which again was singled out for critical scorn. Romantic narratives or half-dreams are represented by "Arabel," in which the speaker falls in love with a prostitute, and the partly realistic "In Michigan," so different incidentally from Hemingway's short story with a similar name. Several local color poems reveal Masters's ability to capture realistic detail. "The Sign," for example, describes an old legal sign creaking in the wind, and "The Loop" has more specific items than Sandburg's much more famous "Chicago," although Masters's tendency to give a longer inventory weakens the general effect.

At least two poems are affectionate tributes to his infant daughters, Marcia and Madeline. Finally, there is the curious poem called "The Star," which pleased many reviewers, although the character of mad Frederick who fell in love with the image of a star in a pond does not seem to be highly compelling. Such themes might suggest that Masters was in a transitional stage between his earlier period of writing in conventional forms about rather hackneyed subjects and his later period when more and more he turned a perceptive eye on the world around him. After all, he was forty-six years of age when he was first identified as the author of the Spoon River portraits. But they also confirm his unwillingness to jettison apprenticeship work or poems written in outmoded mediums, and they justify the charges of uncertain taste which critics flung at him for a quarter of a century. Several reviewers, incidentally, noted the inappropriateness of the title, Songs and Satires, since there were obviously few songs in the book and the satiric note was not predominant.

The Great Valley, also published in 1916, is another miscellany with some 64 poems of varied lengths and subjects written in different metres. It is eloquently dedicated to his paternal grandparents, Squire Davis and Lucinda Masters, "who, close to nature, one in deep religious faith, the other in pantheistic rapture and heroism, lived nearly a hundred years in this land of Illinois." Oddly enough no reviewer identified the dedicatees with the Davis and Lucinda

Matlock whose portraits are among the more memorable ones in Spoon River Anthology. There is a reasonably close relationship between the title of the book and its contents, since many of the poems concern either Chicago or the Illinois background. Indeed, the first eight poems have a certain continuity since they deal with Fort Dearborn and its commandant Captain John Whistler, Lincoln, Douglas, Grant, and Logan. But if Masters's intention was to write a volume specifically about Middle America it is not clearly evident.

Here again is the familiar melange. There are classical or mythological poems, such as "Marsyas" and "Apollo at Pherae," which drew the scorn of most reviewers. Poems addressed to a bombyx and spirochaete exemplify Masters's tendency to introduce scientific subjects into verse. Impressive personal tributes are paid to Theodore Dreiser, John Cowper Powys, and Robert Ingersoll. There are romantic love visions or eulogies of life companions such as "In the Loggia" and "Emily Brosseau: In Church," and an occasional nature poem like "The Desplaines Forest." Masters included one modern antique ballad, "The Search," and three linked sonnets entitled "The Furies." The most impressive poems in the book are either realistic and satiric portraits in the manner of the Spoon River epitaphs or genre scenes and narratives. "Cato Braden" and "Old Piery," despite excessive length, almost belong in the anthology, and dramatic, sardonic tales like "Steam Shovel Cut" show Masters's ability to tell a story compactly and starkly.

Technically the poems illustrate again Masters's tendency to employ various metres. Blank verse, sometimes quite irregular, was a favorite form, free verse is common, sonnets appear, but the poem in stanzaic pattern was most generally used. Although Masters allowed rough lines and various clichés to remain in the published book, the poems of The Great Valley seem less commonplace and certainly less pretentious than those in Songs and Satires. At least the book preserves less evidence of his long apprenticeship. Both volumes attracted attention, but almost invariably the reviews began with the statement that the new collections were less novel and therefore less memorable than Spoon River Anthology.

One of the earliest notices of Songs and Satires appeared in the Yale Review. Here Edward Bliss Reed lamented its obvious lack of life and called it "a curious and disappointing mixture of discordant styles and ideas."1 He also remarked that Masters revealed an exaggerated pessimism and that even a satirist was obligated to see life whole. Among the individual poems "Silence" and "The Cocked Hat" stood out in his mind. Francis Hackett contributed a long review to the New Republic, not all of which was strictly relevant. He praised Masters in general terms as "a great poetic spirit, one of the greatest in the America of our time," and contended that he was one of the first poets to become really articulate in a civilization affected by the machine. Hackett cited several poems as meritorious, notably those celebrating Reedy and Bryan and the bitter little narratives, "In the Car" and "In the Cage." Hackett praised Masters for his technical skill but failed to analyze any of the poems very carefully.2 Raymond M. Alden in the Dial wrote a long negative paragraph in which he said that Masters's trenchant monologues combined some of the qualities of Swift, Whitman, and Shaw but that the poet himself had no style; that is to say, "no consistent medium of expression used with a sense of form, either prosaic or poetic."3 He particularly admired "The Door" but felt that few poems in Songs and Satires approached this. Using a rather singular metaphor, Alden asserted that Masters had a Packard engine in a Ford body!

Two anonymous notices appeared in the middle of 1916. The critic for the Review of Reviews admitted that Masters had some truly lyric qualities, a merit more frequently denied by reviewers, but contended that his real ability lay in portraiture; he called Masters the Sargent among poets.4 A similar tone dominates the Independent's notice. "The Loop" was assailed for its catalogue realism whereas the portraits, even though reminiscent of Spoon River Anthology, showed remarkable skill.5 On the whole, the reviewer could only conclude that Songs and Satires was generally undisciplined and uneven.

The reviewer for the New York Times Book Review expressed very similar opinions.6 In Songs and Satires Masters revealed his deep interest in human beings and in the reality of life whether inspiring or sordid. He was inclined neither to gloss over human weakness nor to withhold sympathy. The critic detected no white heat of passion in Masters's work, without which he said the poet had probably no claim to true greatness, but admitted that Masters showed a mind of singular sincerity and power. As to individual poems, "The Cocked Hat" was a remarkable pen portrait of

Bryan but had not the remotest link with poetry and would have been better written in prose. On the other hand, "So We Grew Together" revealed the poet at his best and the much admired "Silence" deserved all the praise it had been accorded.

Two English reviews of Songs and Satires were grudgingly appreciative of some of Masters's accomplishments but pulled no punches in citing his faults. The London Athenaeum denied categorically that Masters had any theory of poetry at all. He would imitate almost anybody (Browning, Whitman, Longfellow, William Morris), with the result that some of his pieces were comically bad. The worst examples were his attempts to capture the spirit of the ancient ballads. Yet the critic did perceive a certain virility in his work. "Mr. Masters has vigour and imagination, but he will not become a success in Europe until he gets discrimination, and learns to combine beauty with strength."[7] The anonymous critic of the London Times Literary Supplement asked a question which must have puzzled other reviewers: were the poems of this 1916 volume written before or after Spoon River Anthology? They showed talent and an ability to write in many moods, but so often they were crude or merely literary, ranging, as the reviewer put it, from a Malory brought up to date to Mr. Dooley. Masters disliked what might be called diluted morals, yet beneath his superficial cynicism or scorn there existed a true appreciation of innocence and nobility. Certainly, poems like "Silence" and "The Door" were admirable.[8]

It was probably unfortunate for Masters that his collection entitled The Great Valley appeared in the same year as Carl Sandburg's Chicago Poems, since the two books were often bracketed in the same reviews, and generally to Masters's disadvantage. Sandburg's volume was so much rougher, so much more explosive in tone that whatever novelty Masters displayed was quickly overshadowed. Oddly enough, Geddes Smith in the Independent called Masters rather than Sandburg the poet of Chicago and the Middle West who excelled in picturing the sordid and the tragic; he claimed that "few poets have so completely stripped even tragedy of its glamor." But again it was Masters's portraiture that won distinction. Smith selected "Cato Braden" despite its length, because it was a "superb history of a failure," and commended the poet for delineating one man's life as well as the soul of a community.[9] William Aspenwall Bradley, writing in the Dial, also admired "Cato Braden" but contended that it should have been kept to the length of the Spoon River epitaphs. Generally Masters was needlessly discursive and too often tempted into bombast and turgidity (almost like Sandburg, said Bradley). The critic was frankly scornful of Masters's poetry on two counts. Although Masters attempted various technical forms he revealed artistic ineptitude in using all of them. And although he had read a whole library of science and philosophy, he imposed his conglomerate wisdom on his audience in the style of a "popular preacher of semi-literary, pseudo-scientific pretensions."10

An unsigned review in the New York Times complained that Masters in his new volume revealed no deepening of vision, no intensification of poetic skill. Many of the poems, the reviewer remarked, showed a monotonous sameness, while his performance was often marred by haste and carelessness. The poet's ruggedness and power suggested an unusual comparison, however, since the critic felt that Masters might be called a rhythmic Zola. Among the poet's strong merits were his humor, his control of emotion, and his ability to draw character, but even his skill in portraiture was limited by his lack of subtlety. Some individual poems were mentioned as especially commendable: "In the Loggia" for its literary effect and "The Garden" and "The Desplaines Forest" for Masters's success in the expression of a meditative mood. The review concluded with the assertion that the poet was a scientific analyst' who penetrated life to the core.11

In contrast, the Review of Reviews printed a noncommittal note to the effect that The Great Valley was pleasantly American with a strain of constructive nationalism evident throughout its pages. Proof of this would be found specifically in the poems about Fort Dearborn and Captain John Whistler. But words of praise were also found for the portraits of Ingersoll, Dreiser, and Powys, as well as for "Autochthon," that curious poem which linked Darwin, Tennyson, and Lincoln because all three famous figures had the same birth year.12

For his 1918 volume, Toward the Gulf, Masters chose a geographical title which seemed to come in logical sequence after The Great Valley. Whatever structural coherence the book has derives from the epic sweep of the Mississippi River from Lake Itasca to the Gulf of Mexico, the river becoming a symbol for the flood of civilization and the rise of heroes. The title poem, although vapidly rhetorical, collects the human and fluvial tributaries of the

Father of Waters, and Masters weaves in at will poems about places and people with some relevance to the main theme. Nevertheless, the book is again a miscellany. Samson and Delilah, Johnny Appleseed, and Shakespeare on the eve of his death are all the subjects of poems, while Lake Michigan and the streets of Chicago often provide the background for verse tales. In mood as well as in theme there is variety: lyrical description, satire, eulogy, patriotic fervor, idealism. The metrical forms include free verse, blank verse, and several stanzaic arrangements.

A short notice in the Review of Reviews called the title poem epical and commented on Masters's attempt to put into verse the evolution of the hybrid peoples of the Middle West. The book showed a merciless analysis of motives and even a certain inscrutability. Readers were warned that Masters did not write about nightingales in rose gardens, although he did provide pleasant lyrics and even love poems as graceful interludes. The reviewer singled out one notable poem for comment, "Neanderthal," in which Masters measured the great gulf in intelligence between a prehistorical man and the poet Shelley.13

O.W. Firkins in the Nation was unimpressed; he found Masters to be both an unmodern poet and an unpoetic modernist. Spoon River Anthology had shown both concision and restraint, with the poet proving that a cemetery has the advantage of an enclosure. But Toward the Gulf was filled with "copious and unpausing verse" and beauty was even rarer than in some of his previous volumes. Firkins was bored by the jargon of "Dr. Scudder's Clinical Lecture" and insisted that the book abounded in lewdness. Even the Shakespeare whom Masters imagined as giving a monologue in "To-morrow Is My Birthday" was presented as chiefly abdominal. Firkins's chief complaint, voiced so often by critics of Masters, was his lack of artistry. Art, he said, is mostly the conserving of effect; Masters unfortunately disdained to conserve anything, even his hold on the reader.14

Two long reviews used Toward the Gulf as a kind of springboard for general discussion of poetry. Conrad Aiken in the Dial discussed the revolt of contemporary poets against convention.15 The imagists, he pointed out, were primarily lyric poets who experimented with form and color and consequently tried for greater freedom of expression. But poets like Frost and Masters brought to verse almost a new world, "the world of the individual consciousness in its complex entirely." Stated differently, Aiken said that there were two kinds of magics, that which appealed to a sense of beauty and that which appealed to a sense of reality. Shelley might represent the one type, Frost and Masters the other. Aiken claimed that Masters, although he tried to write lyric poetry, was essentially a digger-out of facts relating to human behavior. Thus he was best in narrative verse. Pyschological storytelling was his forte and stressed Masters's annoying unevenness and his faulty sense the medium of poetry required him to check his natural impulse to be discursive and loquacious. Aiken once again stressed Masters's annoying unevenness and his faulty sense of taste. Toward the Gulf contains poems ranging from the downright ludicrous ballad about Launcelot to the well sustained "Arabel." Closer scrutiny of his art, Aiken asserted, would have led Masters to eliminate some poems and to delete such verbal faults as "forgerer" and "disregardless."

A similarly philosophic review was contributed to the New Republic by Edith Franklin Wyatt. She too ventured to discuss imagism and deplored the freedom which gave the imagist poets almost a license to write prosy verse. In Toward the Gulf Masters demonstrated his ability to write various kinds of poetry, poems of place, of opinion, of criticism. The book's most constant characteristic, Miss Wyatt thought, was its realistic presentation of men and women--or of men rather, since Masters's women were usually weaker and paler creations. Stylistically Masters was faulty, being guilty of excessive literalness and tone-deafness. But nevertheless she conceded that he was a poet of genius.16

The variety of the poetry included in Toward the Gulf also impressed Grace Hazard Conklin, who reviewed the book in the Yale Review. Among the collection she observed poems of places, portrait-sketches, even occasional lyrics, and she detected prophetic as well as critical moods. Above all Masters showed power, whether he was writing merciless analysis or expressing his cold fury at the insincerity and smug complacency he saw around him. The reviewer ended her comment with friendly praise for the Johnny Appleseed poem and with the quotation of the final lines as evidence of Masters's success:

A man must fight for the thing he loves, to possess it:
Apples, freedom, heaven, said Peter Van Zylen.17

When Masters assembled another collection of hymns, apostrophes, and monologues--to use the words of an anonymous critic in the Nation--he once more chose a title with regional and symbolic overtones.18 Starved Rock, the volume which appeared in 1919, takes its name from a rocky escarpment on the Illinois River where, according to legend, a band of Illinois Indians, surrounded by their bitter enemies, the Pottawotamies, took refuge and without either food or water perished. It was in the vicinity of Starved Rock, too, that Masters chose the scene of Elenor Murray's death, the focal event in Domesday Book. Again, however, Masters's title promised more poetry of a regional nature than he provided. There are, to be sure, poems about Chicago, and tributes to an oak tree, a house on the hill, and wild water birds suggest a rural Middle Western environment. But Long Island, Washington, and Italy are also chosen settings, while classical and Biblical subjects seem to be favored as much as themes closer home. Like his two preceding collections, Starved Rock is a miscellany, varied in subject matter and metrical form, without any clear pattern. Reviewers raised some of the same objections they had voiced about previous volumes and yet they conceded that Starved Rock contained some striking poems.

One of the earliest reviews was contributed by Marguerite Wilkinson to the New York Times Book Review.19 Miss Wilkinson found Masters a difficult poet to evaluate because he was not selective and his verse lacked basic order. Masters, she thought, inveighed against too many enemies-- Methodists, sabbatarians, Puritans; to him Jehovah, the god of the Jews, was an alien tyrant. He was a thinker who chose verse as his medium and a thinker is naturally more discursive than a singer. For that matter, a novel or an essay might have been a more suitable form for his thought. Miss Wilkinson found frequent evidence of hasty writing and triteness. In her view, one of the best poems in the book was "At Sagamore Hill," the tribute to Theodore Roosevelt in which Masters returned to actuality and personality. This political accolade was worth all the invocations of dead gods long since forgotten.

The Nation critic claimed that Starved Rock was most acceptable when it followed the tone and method of Spoon River Anthology. Masters had established his approach in that memorable book and the vein seemed inexhaustible. He Nevertheless, the poet should not become complacent. He was often too easily satisfied, too inclined also to append a moral to every poem, and he unfortunately showed signs of adopting the role of a prairie seer. Actually, Masters was more credible when he was sifting Spoon River scandal. Another anonymous notice, in the Independent, asserted that although the poems showed little music they were thoughtful. The reviewer warned prospective readers that they might not accept the poet's point of view.[20]

Marjorie Seiffert began her review of Starved Rock with the remark that Masters's stepping stone to fame, Spoon River Anthology, had proved to be a stumbling block since it interfered with his later success. His audience expected succinctness and brevity; he gave his readers longer poems, often overweighted with philosophy. Starved Rock, the reviewer felt, had little beauty but fierce intensity, and she professed to find in the collection a certain coherence among the otherwise unrelated poems because they developed one purpose, the will to know. Miss Seiffert chose the poems about Byron, Poe, and Roosevelt as especially meritorious and expressed the judgment that some of the lyrics in the book, such as "The House on the Hill" and "By the Waters of Babylon," seemed out of place among the narrative and philosophical verse. Nevertheless, she concluded that Starved Rock was "the expression of a profoundly religious soul, a keenly analytical mind, in an eager, passionate human being."[21]

Two other reviews represent the conflicting points of view so often visible in critical judgments of Masters. O. W. Firkins, who generally expressed a negative reaction, felt disinclined to review Starved Rock at all, and chose, rather to review the man.[22] Indulging in the paradoxes that so often marked his critical style, Firkins asserted that Masters was "a man of undoubted ability, though much of his output is less than able. He is even a man of undoubted poetical ability, though much of his ability is not poetic." To support these remarks Firkins then alleged that imperfections of culture, the want of self-discipline, the mixture of assiduity and indolence were all indications of a mind not fully completed by nature. "The mind is not equal to its job; its works are approximations." The reader of Starved Rock, Firkins thought, will neither starve nor feast. There are the usual monologues, only two of which are slimy, some expressions of cosmic philosophy and hazy idealism, and an excellent piece of journalism called "At Sagamore Hill." Occasional but rare lyric passages prove that Masters had moments of true inspiration. Henry A. Lappin's Bookman review, in contrast to Firkins, was not only sympathetic but laudatory. Starved Rock, he claimed, was a somber book with the usual monochords of irony and disillusionment but it also revealed a passionate sincerity. America should be grateful for a poet who could produce the mordant and merciless analyses of the Byron and Poe poems, not to overlook the incomparable portrait of Roosevelt in "At Sagamore Hill." Lappin proclaimed without reservation that Masters was the greatest American poet since Walt Whitman.23

Masters's 1921 volume, The Open Sea, is the most heterogeneous of the collections being discussed in this chapter and contains the fewest memorable poems. Despite the highly adverse biography of Lincoln which he published just ten years later, Masters seemed almost obsessed with the Lincoln story in The Open Sea and devoted half the volume to poems about the president and the Booth family. There is even a play called "The Decision" which ends with the presidential edict to call out the troops following the firing on Fort Sumter. The second half of the book is extremely miscellaneous, with poems on Nebuchadnezzar and Ulysses, a monologue in pidgin English by a Chicago Chinaman who wonders why it took so long for China to hear about "Geesu Kliste," a monody on the death of William Marion Reedy, and a celebration of the Indiana dunes on the southern shore of Lake Michigan. Its shapeless content probably explains, even better than the mediocrity of the verse included, the failure of The Open Sea to attract much attention.

There were few reviews. Agnes Lee Freer, writing in Poetry, a magazine which was generally more friendly to Masters than other periodicals, found it difficult to praise the book. She observed quite correctly that in The Open Sea all sorts and conditions of men spoke out, telling their stories of sordidness or beauty. She also stressed that Masters was here producing an unlocalized Spoon River, with settings which included Indiana, Rome, and Babylon. Masters knew Illinois thoroughly and used his knowledge effectively in the Lincoln poems. But as usual, he seldom filed or polished, with the result that occasional fine lines were often buried among tedious recitative.24 She conceded reluctantly that Masters was still under the shadow of Spoon River Anthology.

Without a cache of older verse to draw upon and with few new poems to include, Masters felt constrained in

1925 to bring together his Selected Poems, a thick volume of 411 pages dedicated to John Cowper Powys. The poet served here as his own editor. Eight books provided the material for the volume; the five collections of miscellaneous verse previously discussed plus Domesday Book (from which he extracted only an independent monologue) and the two Spoon River anthologies. There are nine sections. Dramatic portraits begin the volume and include the familiar sketches of Bryan, Byron, Poe, Reedy, Powys, and Roosevelt. The Great Valley and the City section brings together chiefly poems of places--Chicago, Starved Rock, the Indiana dunes, the Michigan marshes. Stories in verse deal with Tasso, Ulysses, and Johnny Appleseed. The New Apocrypha comes mostly from The Open Sea where eleven poems are grouped under that rubric. Lyrics and sonnets present various lighter pieces and include some uncollected verse. Dithyrambs range from the pretentious invocations to Pentheus and Pallas Athene to the monody on the death of Reedy. Poems of reflection illustrate Masters's interest in science and his addiction to a rather hazy philosophy. The remaining sections are given over to the famous acid portraits, twenty each from the two Spoon River anthologies.

The brief prefatory note calls attention to Masters's problems in selection as well as his concern to represent the quality and variety of his themes to his readers. Otherwise the editor said nothing about the principles which guided his choice of inclusion. He was unfortunately reluctant to eliminate some of the bathetic and imitative early verse. The poem on Helen of Troy still finds a place, as do the feeble imitations of early ballads, the Launcelot poems, and poems notable chiefly for their turgid rhetoric. Certainly Masters would have been wiser here if he had been more willing to listen to and benefit from the criticisms of reviewers. Far too much of the apprenticeship period, far too much of the trite and the prosy, is retained in Selected Poems. It proves once more that the creative writer, whether novelist or poet, is seldom a perceptive critic of his own work.

Reviews of Selected Poems were almost as sparse as those of The Open Sea, possibly because literary editors felt that Masters was overly prolific and had already demanded more than his share of space. One of the few critics to deal with the volume was Harriet Monroe.25 She would not admit that Masters was a one-book man but readily conceded that he was not his own best critic. More rigid editorial discrimination, she thought, would have eliminated most of the poetry from The Open Sea as well as such "freshman classicalities as "Helen of Troy."" But she insisted that anyone who could write poems like "Silence" and "Widow La Rue" and "The Cocked Hat" revealed a rich genius. She claimed that Masters spoke with authority, "in voices epic, reflective, satiric, lyric, humorous," for a whole vast region. Then Miss Monroe repeated her earlier assertions that Masters was distinguished by size and power. In his poetry, she observed, he varied between fiercely satirizing man's inadequacy and profiling great souls at great moments.

John W. Gassner wrote a surprisingly vapid review in which he rather ignored the book but did admit that Selected Poems would be welcome to those readers who considered Masters as the author of only the Spoon River poems. Gassner called the volume an epitome of all the poet's virtues and flaws. Masters revealed a basic dichotomy here: he was both a lyricist of life and a warrior poet. Unfortunately, he did not always sing when he believed that he was singing. Gassner believed that much tedious material in the collection should have been deleted, that more of the Spoon River epitaphs deserved inclusion, and that Masters was probably more eloquent than poetic. 26

Edward Davison sounded a note in the Saturday Review of Literature which became more and more familiar in the later critical evaluations of Masters's verse. 27 Davison censured Masters for being too prolific. In ten years, he estimated, Masters had written (published would have been a more accurate term) some two thousand pages of poetry, a quantity so great that he had already outdistanced Tennyson, Wordsworth, and Milton. The obvious result was that the verse was thin to an extreme. "Haste has taken the edge away from his rhythms and language: his poetry is traced on sand instead of being engraved on brass." Davison did not fail to ascribe certain merits to Masters's work, among them eloquence, vitality, variety, and forcefulness; but he insisted that the writer was not the master of his medium. Masters was never celebrated for verbal beauty but here he was also guilty of crudeness and stylistic infelicities. The critic reiterated the old objection that much of what Masters published as poetry could better have been expressed in prose. One hundred pages rather than two thousand pages might have more accurately represented Masters's poetic achievement.

In the years following 1925 Masters turned his attention to larger themes to which he accorded dramatic and narrative treatment. His first venture into this field had already appeared in 1920 as Domesday Book. Further collections of fugitive and occasional verse would not appear until the next decade.

Notes

1. Edward Bliss Reed, "Recent American Verse," Yale Review (January, 1917), 6: 417-422.

2. F[rancis] H[ackett], "The New Generation," New Republic (April 29, 1916), 6: 354-356.

3. Raymond M. Alden, "Recent Poetry," Dial (July 15, 1916), 61: 64.

4. Review of Reviews (May, 1916), 53: 632.

5. Independent (July 3, 1916), 87: 28-29.

6. "Songs and Satires by Mr. Masters," New York Times Book Review (May 21, 1916), 220.

7. London Athenaeum (November, 1916), No. 4611, 529.

8. "The Poet of Spoon River," London Times Literary Supplement (September 21, 1916), No. 75, 451.

9. Geddes Smith, "Four Pioneer Poets," Independent (December 25, 1916), 88: 533-538.

10. William Aspenwall Bradley, "Four American Poets," Dial (December 14, 1916), 61: 528-532.

11. New York Times Review of Books (January 7, 1917), 1-2.

12. Review of Reviews (December, 1916), 54: 674.

13. Review of Reviews (May, 1918), 57: 554.

14. O. W. Firkins, "Assorted Poets," Nation (October 26, 1918), 107: 488-489.

Some Intermediate Collections

15. Conrad Aiken, "The Two Magics," <u>Dial</u> (May 9, 1918), 64: 447-449.

16. Edith Franklin Wyatt, <u>New Republic</u> (August 24, 1918), 16: 114-118.

17. Grace Hazard Conklin, "What Is Poetry?" <u>Yale Review</u> (January, 1919), n.s., 8: 432-438.

18. "Low Tide in Spoon River," <u>Nation</u> (April 24, 1920), 110: 557.

19. Marguerite Wilkinson, "Mr. Masters Echoes a Tragic Muse," <u>New York Times Book Review</u> (March 7, 1920), 4.

20. <u>Independent</u> (October 9, 1920), 104: 65.

21. Marjorie A. Seiffert, <u>Poetry: A Magazine of Verse</u> (June, 1920), 16: 151-156.

22. O. W. Firkins, "Vachel Lindsay, Edgar Lee Masters, and Others," <u>Review</u> (May 15, 1920), 2: 519-520.

23. Henry A. Lappin, "Poetry, Verse, and Worse," <u>Bookman</u> (April, 1920), 51: 211-216.

24. Agnes Lee Freer, "Spoon River to the Open Sea," <u>Poetry: A Magazine of Verse</u> (December, 1922), 21: 154-158.

25. H[arriet] M[onroe], "In Bardic Robes," <u>Poetry: A Magazine of Verse</u> (March, 1927), 29: 336-342.

26. John Waldhorn Gassner, "A Warrior Poet," <u>New York Herald Tribune Books</u> (November 22, 1925), 2: 10, 15.

27. Edward Davison, "A Too Prolific Poet," <u>Saturday Review of Literature</u> (December 26, 1925), 2: 443-44.

CHAPTER 5

DOMESDAY BOOK

Although Edgar Lee Masters had always intended to write a novel about a small Middle Western community, it is unlikely that he was working with a preconceived plan when he began to pour his Spoon River epitaphs into Reedy's _Mirror_ in the spring of 1914. It is true that "The Hill," which begins the 1915 anthology, and five of the sketches which were published originally on May 29, 1914, occupy the opening pages of the celebrated volume itself. But it would be hard to detect any pattern here. As Masters continued to contribute the poems to the _Mirror_, some kind of arrangement undoubtedly occurred to him, yet it was only after he had written enough of the epitaphs to demonstrate their interrelationships and to group them into categories that any specific order became feasible. It is also possible that the lusty sinners, the predators, the misfits, the derelicts attracted him first and insisted on being given their places in the graveyard before he found room for the mystics and idealists. At any rate, it is easy to argue that the present arrangement of the Spoon River speakers was arrived at somewhat accidentally, fitting as it may seem to most readers today. The genesis of _Domesday Book_, on the other hand, was somewhat different.

The preceding chapter has demonstrated that Masters, after the appearance of the anthology, was in a military sense consolidating his position. In other words he was reviewing his earlier work, winnowing the mass of his previous verse, and bringing forth between new covers what he deemed to be his most impressive poems. To put it still another way, Masters was exploiting his sudden fame with the hope that the public might be induced to buy other books from his pen. When he finally turned to a genuinely new theme, a long narrative poem about a single episode with incredibly numerous ramifications which would eventually extend far beyond Spoon River and even Illinois to the other side of the Atlantic Ocean, he had to devise a firm structure. He could no longer depend on improvisation or random choice. In a sense he was motivated by dual stimuli: his own past experience and his reading.

Both Spoon River Anthology and Domesday Book were written in Chicago, where Masters maintained his law office in the Loop. He later explained in an article contributed to the Nation that he was thrilled by "the psychical cyclone of that place, constantly teased to record in verse the stories of the men who had built the city" as well as the tales of colorful and unique characters who figured in the newspaper reports he read daily.[1] When it came time to work on Domesday Book he rented a room in a tower overlooking the waterfront and Michigan Avenue, "from which I could see the boats and the gulls and hear the whir of the thousands passing on the pavement a hundred feet below me; and these surroundings stirred my thinking and imagining."

The actual impulse to write the story came from another recollection. Masters recorded in his autobiography that while riding a bus down New York's Fifth Avenue on one occasion, he recalled scenes in his father's law office back in Lewistown when he and some chosen cronies would discuss logic and philosophy. The memory became seminal.[2]

I imagined a group of four or five young men similarly engaged as we were in discussion and study. One of them, a skeptic and misanthrope, committed suicide. The others came into the room and looked at the tragic scene. When they took in hand to report what they saw they differed from one another in many details, some important, some trivial, just as I had seen witnesses do in the cases that I saw my father try. They also gave varying and contradictory analyses of the suicide's character, and even of his physical appearance. I have observed that few people can remember the color of the eyes of their friends and acquaintances, something that I always take note of with particular care.

Here then was the nucleus of a narrative: a striking event, witnesses to confirm what had happened, and conflicting testimony because of the general inability of people to see things fully, to remember clearly, and to report accurately what they thought they knew about the persons involved. Given such a situation the narrator could range far afield, investigating personal relationships, weighing circumstantial evidence, speculating about motives, diagnosing actions. Moreover, there was virtually no limit to the number and kinds of people who might be involved in what seemed on the surface to be a simple episode.

The Illinois background was again important to Masters, but a literary source also impinged here. About the year of Masters's birth Robert Browning had published The Ring and the Book, a long poetic narrative about a Roman murder case. The Italian story is full of intrigue, matrimonial deceit, melodramatic flights, court accusations, and murders, with the Pope eventually pronouncing the death penalty against the guilty husband, Count Guido Franceschini, who first married Pompilia and then tried to get rid of her. Despite the violent action it was Browning's skill in handling his material, and especially his success in allowing various informants to reveal themselves while giving evidence, that insured the poem's success. Browning's heroine Pompilia is surely a long way removed from the Elenor Murray of Domesday Book, and an Illinois county coroner can hardly be compared as a figure of authority with the Roman pontiff. Moreover, Elenor Murray is not a murder victim but dies of syncope soon after she is found on the shore of the Illinois River. But Masters, here more than ever the lawyer, calls upon a variety of witnesses as Browning did and develops the story from a multiple point of view, his intention being in the process to take a "census spiritual" of all America.

Masters never admitted his obligation to The Ring and the Book. Indeed, in his autobiography he averred that he completed his own poem before he had read a line of Browning's work and even added, "perhaps before I ever heard of it."3 But the denial seems a bit disingenuous. At any rate, readers and critics were quick to find similarities between The Ring and the Book and Domesday Book, and hardly a review appeared which did not suggest some relationship between the two works. Nevertheless, the later poem is not slavish imitation. Without a basic plan Masters simply could not have written a narrative poem of 396 pages. His methodology he conceivably adapted from the English poet; his material was strikingly different.

The plot of Domesday Book is simple enough. Masters's use of a single event as the substratum of a series of interlocking narratives is reminiscent of Theodore Dreiser's successful magnifying of a newspaper report about a drowning in a New York lake into a long novel, An American Tragedy. One day a rabbit hunter, Barrett Bays, comes upon a female figure lying on the shore of the Illinois River a mile above Starved Rock. He immediately recognizes her as Elenor Murray, whom he had known intimately in the past. He picks her up instead of allowing her to remain in a recumbent position, only to discover that she is dead. The inquest of the coroner's jury, announced at the town of LeRoy on August 7, 1919, frees Bays of any complicity in her death and the case is closed. These facts are the substance of Masters's poem.

But Coroner William Merival, obliged to interrupt a Michigan fishing trip to investigate the death, is not satisfied with the circumstantial evidence. Elenor Murray was a local girl, known to many, the daughter of a LeRoy druggist. She was bright, attractive, somewhat impetuous and willful. Masters portrays her as a free spirit, eager and ambitious, determined to break away from conventional life. She works as a teacher, a cashier, and finally as a nurse in France during World War I. She has various emotional affairs, including one with Bays, and figures in the breakup of at least one marriage. Merival knows much of this background and is determined to find out what impelled Elenor Murray to lead the life she chose. He carefully assembles a coroner's jury and summons witnesses. The major part of Domesday Book is given over to their testimony about Elenor's life and character: among the speakers are Mr. and Mrs. Murray, the parents; a teacher, Alma Bell; the piano instructor, Gottlieb Gerald; an employee of Elenor's grandfather, John Scofield; a priest, a neurologist, the sheriff, the governor. All contribute facts or speculations about the girl's life, and eventually a composite picture is painted. In the meanwhile Masters achieved a kind of cross-section, not as sharply focused as that in Spoon River Anthology but extensive and wide-ranging. In Merival's words,

Shall not I as a coroner in America,
Inquiring of a woman's death, make record
Of lives which have touched hers, what lives she
    touched;
And how her death by surest logic touched
This life or that, was cause of causes, proved
The event that made events?[4]

Domesday Book was widely reviewed, sometimes in conjunction with Mitch Miller since both poem and novel appeared in the same year, but most critics expressed reservations about it. Masters was generally given credit for the breadth and vision of his initial conception and for his skill in handling the structure. But there was virtually unanimous agreement that the poem was too long, the length made even more obvious by repetition, that the reader was not held by the narrative, and that the chosen poetic medium was pedestrian. At the beginning of his work Masters had decided that the poem was inappropriate for a continuous narrative circling around a single happening. Thus he chose instead to use blank verse, a form which he had employed eighteen years earlier in the drama Maximilian. In the eyes of most critics it was not a happy selection.

Carl Van Doren was one of the first reviewers to couple Mitch Miller and Domesday Book, although in his review in the Nation he discussed each book independently.[5] Van Doren was impressed by the scheme and machinery of the poem in which Coroner Merival, a philosophical amateur as a sleuth, attempted to ferret out all the facts about the death of Elenor Murray. He was not averse to Masters's effort to make the work an allegory of America, but he felt that too much time was spent in arraigning the inhibitions of the society in which the girl lived. Masters, according to Van Doren, could hate like no other American poet but often failed to transmute his hates into poetry, with the result that they remained a sullen mass of animosity. The critic also objected to the turgid learning and scientific speculations which on the whole remained undigested. Yet he was willing to concede Masters certain strong merits: "the sinews of enormous power, a greedy gusto for life, a wide imaginative experience, tumultuous uprushes of emotion and expression, a restless if undisciplined intelligence." This was no authentic masterpiece, however; the parts simply did not contribute to an impressive whole.

Two interesting reviews appeared in December, 1920. Padraic Colum wrote in the New Republic that Domesday Book was a veritable "man of lawe's tale," a mixture of satire and dramatic poetry which has the immediate interest of a novel.[6] He praised Masters's boldness in undertaking such a formidable task but at the same time complained that the poem was in a sense unfinished. The story did indeed reach a conclusion, but many parts were left incomplete and some characters (notably Elenor Murray's mother) seemed incompletely revealed. Colum was aware of the parallel with Browning's earlier poem and pointed out that Domesday Book lacked a commanding character. He also expressed a moral judgment, commenting that all the people in the poem showed an extraordinary willfulness and virtually no moral discipline at all. Elenor Murray gave herself to two lovers with no worries about either chastity or constancy. Colum felt that she had reality but no appeal.

Oliver M. Sayler, in the Freeman, thought Masters should be praised for his willingness to avoid further floundering in minor verse forms and to find a new literary mould. He approved of the choice of Browning as a model and of the attempt to show the links between Elenor Murray's life and the lives of others. But he criticized Masters for not being sufficiently selective; moreover the poet was all too willing to express "some of his own economic and psychological and philosophical hobbies" at inappropriate times. The reader was fortunately spared some of the excursions into mediaeval or classical periods that disfigured a few of Masters's earlier poems. Nevertheless, much of Domesday Book was hopelessly prosaic. It could easily have been cut to half its size by excision or compression. 7

Several brief and anonymous notices appeared early in 1921. The Dial called Domesday Book a poem which was simply "a magnificent, but badly written novel." The North American Review claimed that Masters got his material not from a book, like Browning, but from newspapers, and was uncertain about the poet's intention. "The fact remains that this extraordinarily long, extremely pedestrian, excessively realistic poem does seem to be trying, and insistently trying, to say something." The reviewer commented on the unusualness of a poet including in his work the details of a post-mortem examination. The Independent credited Masters with a stirring idea but complained about the dullness of the result. Masters inserted scientific analysis and clinical psychology but failed to relieve such stodgy material with the music of phrase or metre. 8 It becomes apparent at once that most of the early reviewers felt the excessive length of Domesday Book was its most serious flaw.

Louis Untermeyer, generally more hospitable to new poetry than his contemporary critics were, denied that Domesday Book had any lyric fire. 9 He stated bluntly that "Masters's chief equipment is a brooding seriousness, a dogged and frequently flagellating honesty, an intensive analy-sis that is, at base, a spiritual seeking," and called the book a frank imitation of Browning. Masters's stiff and monotonous style was another source of irritation to Unter-meyer. Indeed he was one of the few reviewers to observe Masters's failure to differentiate his various speakers in voice and tone. Although the many characters in _Domesday Book_ represent basic differences in age, background, educa-tion, and social position, they all sound very much alike. Moreover, they are inconsistent in their language, both Mrs. Murray and the sheriff, for example, shifting without ex-planation or need from the colloquial to the rhetorical. Untermeyer, nevertheless, granted Masters great power and suggested that his future might yet prove as spectacular as his past.

Harriet Monroe could not fail to notice the appear-ance of a major work by Masters and could not help being sympathetic to a poet whom she had encouraged and pub-lished previously. Still she was cautious. She began her _Poetry_ review by pointing out that Masters was both a law-yer and a poet.[10] His legal work had developed in him a talent for shrewd and imaginative cross-examination; his poetic experience had given him a comprehensive and sym-pathetic view of life from the inside. But she confessed that hundreds of pages of a ten-syllable iambic line did not guarantee a poem; many of the monologues in _Domesday Book_ she found dull because of their undistinguished style, and she thought some of the less relevant passages might have been deleted. But Miss Monroe contended that the po-em was not a mere photograph but a transfigured vision with certain viable characters. Elenor Murray, hardly a heroine of size, probably failed to be a convincing symbol of America's tireless searching or immense achievement. Still, the poem possessed immensity of scope and power. She called it finally a modern tale of psychological adven-ture, similar to Browning's story but contemporary rather than mediaeval.

The review by O. W. Firkins in the _Weekly Review_ was more concerned with structure than with style.[11] In-deed, the critic denied that the book was really poetry and remarked wrily that "The very blank verse has a shy effect of hoping it isn't in the way." Firkins found the first por-tion of the book interesting and all of it readable. Then he proceeded to define the four strands of plot: a detective story like _The Moonstone_ or _The Ring and the Book_; a study

of the cause and both a summary and chronicle of the impact of Elenor Murray's death; a rough and slight criticism
of American life; and a fringe of metaphysics. Masters constructed his narrative as a series of depositions given in the
order of their reception and perusal by the coroner; thus
Elenor Murray's life could not be told consecutively. The
interlineations, as Firkins put it, "grow in number, shrink
in bulk, and wane in clarity." He did not find Elenor Murray a very likable heroine and claimed that she seemed to
be propelled toward the goals of lust and greed. Not many
critics even in 1921 would have agreed that the book was
steeped or sodden in sex, nor would they have admitted that
the sexual freedoms claimed by the poet were large. But
Firkins was not the only reviewer to argue that Masters often stated problems without venturing solutions. And his objection to Elenor Murray as a symbolic figure was sustained
by many other writers.

Thus C. E. Lawrence, writing in the London Bookman, also objected to Masters's presentation of his heroine
and commented that she was particularly unconvincing to an
English reader.12 He thought the parallel was quite un-
necessary. Lawrence was hardly ecstatic in his praise of
Domesday Book but he claimed that Masters's rebellion
against hypocrisy and conventionality in what he termed "this
brave poem" would attract readers. While hardly equal to
the memorable anthology, Domesday Book was "a strength-
ening, frank challenge to the conventionalists: it is packed
with lucid wisdom, is rich with human sympathy, and has
occasional passages of music which prove the poet." Lawrence, it might be noted, said nothing about the poem's
metrical form or style.

The most hostile early review was definitely that of
Stuart Sherman in the Yale Review.13 Sherman bluntly
termed Elenor Murray a whore and asserted that if she had
kindly, religious, and riotous moods she certainly had no
principles. Masters was trained as a lawyer, Sherman reminded his readers, and showed evidence of having browsed
through a large amount of miscellaneous literature. But
when he indulged in speculative reasoning he evinced all the
sophistication, all the intellectual capacity of the late Anna
Held (once a favorite star of the musical stage). Sherman
could hardly restrain his contempt: "this ponderous inquest
impresses me as much ado about slush." He reached the
peak of his attack on Masters by comparing him with his
favorite bête noire, the serious lumbering work of a certain

Indiana novelist (i.e., Theodore Dreiser).

An anonymous review in the London New Statesman corroborated Sherman's diatribe. The critic began his notice by remarking that much contemporary English verse was dull and that most American verse lacked artistry. Then he added: "Mr. Edgar Lee Masters has the vices of the English school and of the American school, for his verse is flat like most of the former and crude with much of the latter."14 He admitted that Spoon River Anthology showed a certain nimbleness, but insisted that Domesday Book unhappily exemplified "unquenchable garrulity" and languished from both lack of matter and excess of speech. Quotations from both Browning and Marlowe supported his decision. The reviewer ignored everything in his review save Masters's style; he either misunderstood the poet's intention or he was unimpressed by the poem as a narrative.

The English critic Edmund Gosse pointed out that Domesday Book was longer than Wordsworth's Excursion but that it had some sterling merits and was readable although definitely not a masterpiece.15 The dullness and wretchedness of the provincial scene as Masters described it reminded him of George Crabbe, an analogy which occurred to few other critics. Gosse was impressed by the variety and vividness of Masters's portraits in the poem, even though all were failures in life, with merely the veneer of respectability. Gosse was not offended by the characterization of Elenor Murray but he claimed that her lovers were ludicrously numerous and her polyandry rather grotesque. It seemed to him that Masters's basic theme was that youth's happiness was undermined by having to conceal the tortures and risks of sex.

In contrast to the reviews in the literary journals Florence Fleisher contributed to Survey an analysis of Domesday Book from quite a different point of view. Masters's book, she contended, had generally been considered as a poem without real poetry, as a novelty without real novelty, and as narrative dealing with willful, undisciplined people. Actually it was not a work of art at all and should not be judged in this fashion; it was primarily social diagnosis. Masters simply presented his criticism of life in America in a way which would be unavailable to the social philosopher--by means of a mystery plot. The revelation of Elenor Murray's life and death impinged on many people and produced corresponding comment. "Some of the best passages in the book are these letters, editorials and discussions of characters outside the story." And then Miss Fleisher added a comment which now seems clairvoyant: the coroner's jury, she thought, offered a fine opportunity. It took Masters himself almost a decade to realize what an opportunity that was.16

Nine years after Domesday Book, Masters returned to the story of Elenor Murray in another blank verse narrative which he termed an epilogue to the original. The Fate of the Jury, published in 1929, is less than half the length of Domesday Book and has a quite different focus, although the reader is continually aware of the basic story. As a result of the inquest into the death of the girl the six jurors and the coroner decide that they should examine their own lives and grasp the "central clew" to their existence. Three of the stories are given in detail and reveal the destinies of the speakers: David Borrow, opportunist and publicist, writes a letter; Samuel Ritter confesses to the coroner and disappears, probably a suicide; Winston Marion, a newspaper editor, gives his written confession while on his deathbed. Of the other three, the Reverend Maiworm talks to the coroner and then, with Llewellyn George and Isaac Newfeldt, "drifted off at last, passed out forgotten." Coroner William Merival's own story provides the enveloping action of the narrative. He, lonely and restless, seeks solace in the company of Arielle, an attractive young widow. Eventually, despite warning signs which he disregards, he marries her, only to find that there is hereditary insanity in her family; shortly after the marriage she goes mad and he cares for her until she dies. Thus, in a sense, Merival's ill-fated romance substitutes for the inquest into Elenor Murray's death as the central plot theme.

The Fate of the Jury was not widely reviewed and could not be entirely divorced from its predecessor. But even though it shows some of the usual disadvantages of a sequel it had a fairly hospitable reception. Most reviewers thought that it was generally readable and conceded that it was relatively free from the platitudes and prolixity that disfigured much of Domesday Book. It never gained a wide audience, however, and has been little read since its first appearance.

Conrad Aiken, generally a harsh critic of Masters, called The Fate of the Jury a first-rate story and even a revelation of the American scene.17 He claimed that it was packed with detail and that the characters had actuality. To him the poem was highly readable. The defects that he could not fail to observe were old flaws in Masters's work: loose and prosaic lines, the belief that prose chopped up into ten-syllable lines became immediately poetic, the bad taste that permitted pretention and empty rhetoric. Horace Gregory, in the New Republic, first bowed in the direction of Domesday Book, which he pronounced a classic of its kind even though it sprawled through miles of blank verse which was really only crippled prose. In The Fate of the Jury, however, lacked a true catharsis. In The Fate of the Jury Masters provided a sequel in which he allowed the jurors to find meaning in their own lives. Gregory even felt that the later poem had more true poetry in it than the earlier one. Still, The Fate of the Jury ended in a minor key and thus became a diminutive coda to a more important work. 18

Louis Untermeyer reviewed Masters's poem together with Robinson's Cavender's House, and found the latter infinitely superior. His review concentrated on Masters's defects as a poet and said virtually nothing about the story or its characters. The Fate of the Jury, he declared, showed little control over words and "the syllables that should condense in tone and shapeliness are merely sawed-off into rude pentameter lengths." 19 An anonymous reviewer in the New York Times Book Review also compared Masters's poem with Robinson's and conceded that Masters was directly and indirectly more of a preacher and far less of an artist. Yet he found some compensation, for he claimed that in Masters's "nervous verse there is that which will appeal more widely than Robinson's calm." 20 The reviewer believed that the narratives founded on the episodes in The Fate of the Jury were less important than the moral derived from them, much of which was expressed by Coroner Merival when he pontificated on the enormous waste of life in America. As a result the poem offered a reading of the nation which went far below the surface. Frank Ernest Hill in another newspaper review declared that The Fate of the Jury was less dramatic and less moving than its predecessor but he wrote in a laudatory tone. Hill made the usual objection to the poetic medium chosen: "The rhythm of his verse gaps and sags and relaxes in a recitative that is prosodically monotonous." But he admitted readily that Masters had a gift for drawing people and for establishing their reality against a recognizable background. 21

One of the most interesting reviews was contributed

by Eda Lou Walton to the Nation.[22] She began by observing that the 1920's had seen an extraordinary revival of interest in long narrative poems. For decades the form had seemed archaic and then all of a sudden such admired poets as Robinson, Frost, and Jeffers had successfully employed it while Stephen Vincent Benét's John Brown's Body had become a great popular favorite. She admitted reservations about the blank verse which was the poetic form commonly adopted for the narratives. Certainly it was not the blank verse of Shakespeare or of Milton. She felt that most writers were actually telling their stories in unrhymed iambic pentameter. In The Fate of the Jury Masters followed his own tradition of being more of a lawyer, psychologist, and storyteller than a poet but the result was extraordinarily good. Miss Walton called the book not only interesting but "an intricate weaving of tale into tale, an account of lesbianism, masochism, and duplicity such as Jeffers himself might, very differently, have used." To her The Fate of the Jury proved that Masters did not always suffer from a heavy touch and that he could sometimes write creditable blank verse.

Masters went on to write other long narrative poems. Indeed, between 1926 and 1934 he published six, two of them dealing with Civil War themes and one with a boyhood companion of Lincoln whom he traced into later years. But none of these attracted much attention, whether they told the story of Jack Kelso or of Robert E. Lee. In this genre Domesday Book remained the poet's greatest achievement.

Notes

1. ELM, "The American Background," Nation (August 26, 1925), 121: 226-229.

2. ELM, Across Spoon River, 368.

3. Ibid., 369.

4. ELM, Domesday Book (New York, 1920), 20-21.

5. C[arl] V[an] D[oren]. Nation (November 17, 1920), 111: 566.

6. Padraic Colum, "A Man of Lawe's Tale," New Republic (December 29, 1920), 25: 148-149.

7. Oliver M. Sayler, "Back to Spoon River," Freeman (December 22, 1920), 2: 3577.

8. Dial (March, 1921), 70: 352; North American Review (February, 1921), 213: 286-287; Independent (March 12, 1921), 105: 277-278.

9. Louis Untermeyer, "Lyric Fire," Bookman (January, 1921), 52: 363-364.

10. H[arriet] M[onroe], "A Census Spiritual," Poetry: A Magazine of Verse (July, 1921), 18: 214-218.

11. O. W. Firkins, "The Coroner Glimpses America," Weekly Review (January 5, 1921), 4: 15.

12. C. E. Lawrence, "Domesday Book," London Bookman (August, 1921), 60: 216-217.

13. Stuart P. Sherman, "Poetic Personalities," Yale Review (April, 1921), 10: 636-637.

14. "An American Poet," New Statesman (July 2, 1921), 17: 362.

15. Edmund Gosse, More Books on the Table (London, 1923), 351-358.

16. Florence Fleisher, "Behold Me As America," Survey (April 2, 1921), 46: 13.

17. Conrad Aiken, Bookman (May, 1929), 69: 323.

18. Horace Gregory, "Weeds Over Bronze," New Republic (August 7, 1929), 59: 322.

19. Louis Untermeyer, "Essential Robinson," Saturday Review of Literature (May 11, 1929), 5: 995-996.

20. "Mr. Masters Writes an Epilogue to 'Domesday Book,'" New York Times Book Review (April 21, 1929), 4, 20.

21. Frank Ernest Hill, "The Great Scene," New York Herald Tribune Books (April 28, 1929), 5.

22. Eda Lou Walton, "Concerning Narrative Verse," Nation (July 17, 1929), 129: 72.

CHAPTER 6

DRAMATIC VERSE NARRATIVES

Masters wrote poetry throughout his life and published at a prodigious rate, to the consternation even of his admirers. At intervals he would collect the short poems that he had contributed to such diverse periodicals as Poetry, the American Mercury, Dial, Commonweal, and the Century, add enough unpublished material to make a volume, and dump the result on a sagging market. Miscellanies like Invisible Landscapes (1935), Poems of People (1936), and Illinois Poems (1941) were certainly compiled in this manner. But the most ambitious poetical projects of the period before and after 1930 took the form of long dramatic narratives which gradually failed to elicit the attention even of reviewers. In the eleven-year span from 1926 to 1937, even without counting The Fate of the Jury, Masters published no less than seven dramatic poems, each of substantial length. During the same period, incidentally, Masters also produced his two final novels, his controversial book on Lincoln, biographies of Twain, Whitman, and Vachel Lindsay, and his own autobiography.

Of the seven dramatic poems, the first two, Lee and Jack Kelso, received the widest discussion, although Lee confused reviewers and Jack Kelso was generally criticized for its tedious length. Lee, a Dramatic Poem appeared in 1926 and was dedicated to Percy Grainger, a dedication which possibly implied that Masters hoped readers would find music inherent in its lines. Divided into four acts and written in blank verse which is often rough and pretentious, the poem follows the biography of Robert E. Lee from his anguished decision to resign his commission in the Union Army in order to fight for Virginia, through Gettysburg and Appomattox, to his quiet years as president of Washington College (now Washington and Lee University) and his death.

Speaking characters include Lee and his wife, assorted minor figures like a mountaineer, a soldier, and a farmer, and personified abstractions such as Virginia and the Republic. There are also two shadowy figures known as Ariman-ius and Ormund who function as a kind of chorus or serve to escort Lee at critical points.

Three anonymous notices of the dramatic poem were somewhat less than enthusiastic. The Independent made the usual comment that Masters had not surpassed himself since the Spoon River epitaphs were published and claimed that they had more genuine drama than the whole of Lee. The choral scene which prefaced the work was only a faint imitation of Greek classical style and the poet in general showed little talent for the grandiose sphere. The reviewer conceded that the verse was balanced, sonorous, and often beautiful in itself but objected to the artificial elevation of the narrative.[1] The New Republic agreed that Masters had no real talent for the grand manner. Lee was not only a long and turgid dramatic poem but was rather suggestive of a community masque. Masters's muse, which descended spectacularly among the Middle Western villagers and lent them eloquence, failed conspicuously here, while the blank verse and choral odes of the poem were like so much cast-iron.[2] The critic for the Nation took a somewhat different tack. He pointed out that the poem was less about Lee than about liberty and that the revered leader of the Confederate armies became a symbol of the free soul battling vainly to retain the conditions of its freedom. Indeed, the Civil War in Masters's poem dramatized the basic conflict between the old way of life and a new technique of tyranny, namely, industrialism. The reviewer said little about either characters or poetic style but claimed that Masters's poem was an addition of genuine depth and power to American literature.[3]

This was the point of view also expressed by Mark Van Doren in the New York Herald Tribune Books. Van Doren carefully avoided giving any opinion about the verse, the characters, and the action or lack of it. He also admitted that he had read better dramatic poems and that Masters's work showed his customary lack of polish. Nevertheless, he was impressed by the ideas in the poem. Masters, in his view, showed an admirable command of the issues and the history involved, as well as a Jeffersonian passion for individual liberty. The poem was not concerned with slavery and abolitionism at all but with the encroachment of the North on the South through the new industrialism. Lee feared the arrival of machinery, feared the increasing power of money; his decision to fight for his state rather than for the Union was motivated by fear of worse things to come. Van Doren argued that Masters's dramatic poem was full of ideas and that it might have been a superior piece of art with fewer of them.[4]

These comments have one thing in common. None of the reviewers found any drama in what purported to be a dramatic poem and none of them thought that Masters succeeded in characterizing any of the dramatic personae. Masters was simply using a conventional literary form as a medium for deeply felt ideas. In Jack Kelso, on the other hand, he dealt more specifically with a single figure, but without greater success.

With this five-act dramatic poem of 1928 Masters returned to the Lincoln country of his youth for setting and plot. Jack Kelso is a fisherman, a bookish dreamer, a companionable idler who is represented by Masters as the friend and literary advisor of the youthful Lincoln. He is also something of a poet. In his own words,

He was a worthless, wandering dunce
Who often tried his hand at rhyme;
Invented masques, you understand,
Great masks that hid the actors' faces.[5]

But early in the narrative both Lincoln and Jack Kelso leave New Salem, the one to achieve great eminence and political martyrdom, the other to roam aimlessly west and east until he finally returns to the Sangamon Valley to die. In the later pages Jack Kelso is little more than a medium for Masters to comment on the evils of American society.

John T. Frederick was convinced that the protagonist was a failure as a character in a drama. By a larger criterion, "Jack Kelso lacks the illusion of reality without attaining the less immediate significance of symbol and idea which its material might make possible." Lyric passages, to be sure, did appear in the book but unfortunately Masters was less a dramatic poet "than a violent, sometimes cruelly just and effective, sometimes rather tiresome, scold." The reader, Frederick pointed out, was expected to follow the career of Jack Kelso as a man but instead was given a series of diatribes against Masters's old scapegoats: imperialism, prohibition, blue laws, Methodism. Years ago, the critic recalled, he had read Masters's early poetic drama Maximilian; he recognized no evidence of increased dramatic power in Jack Kelso.6

Very much the same criticism was expressed by J. Dana Tasker in Outlook. To him Jack Kelso was "history after a fashion."7 The book wandered episodically, like the protagonist himself, through a galaxy of names, people, and places and got nowhere, but Jack Kelso was never a convincing figure. Furthermore, Masters was completely unsuccessful in trying to differentiate his characters by their speech or idiom: Lincoln, Douglas, Kit Carson all spoke alike, a row of so many masked figures. A brief notice in the Dial also called attention to Masters's quaint and sardonic commentary upon American history but found little in the narrative poem to commend otherwise.8

Llewellyn Jones's review was ironic and almost patronizing.9 He thought that Jack Kelso began well enough with its picture of Illinois pioneers, but he believed that Masters had committed a cardinal error in allowing both Jack Kelso and his poem to wander far from the original prairies. A hopeless and hapless wanderer who failed to understand Lincoln, Kelso becomes a vehicle of rather inept social criticism. Jones refrained from commenting on either the poetic qualities or the special merits of the narrative. This was also the attitude of Harriet Monroe in a review which she entitled "Unachieved."10 She questioned Masters's judgment in even attempting a long meditative poem in dialogue and asserted that Kelso never became the figure of myth that Masters probably intended. She concluded somewhat sadly about her old friend and contributor that he was the most unequal poet of his rank in the country, yet she insisted that even in his failures there was a certain magnificence.

Leon Whipple's Survey notice of Jack Kelso commented on the sudden vogue of long poems dwelling on the American scene and the American past and ranging from Stephen Vincent Benét's John Brown's Body, an historical pageant, to Carl Sandburg's paean to the American earth, Good Morning, America. Masters, the critic thought, had attempted drama and succeeded only in writing pale allegory. He also criticized the work for being diffuse and for failing to characterize the people, "until they become figures in a mural, their words the inscriptions on memorial urns."11 John Carter reviewed Jack Kelso with greater acerbity. The

protagonist, according to Carter, was a Yankee Tyl Eulen-
spiegel, a Dante in homespun, wandering through the in-
fernos of American life. Masters, through his alter ego
Jack Kelso, expressed his views about many aspects of the
national scene but seldom escaped reiterated didacticism.
Moreover, the poet held only the loosest of reins over his
creation, with the result that the verse was rough and often
crude, some lines being artlessly clumsy, others little more
than turgid ranting. Paradoxically, however, Masters was
also capable of producing some genuine songs, "charming
lyrics of impeccable form and real beauty of expression."
Carter concluded that Masters had never really left the
Spoon River cemetery and that his muse still wore cypress
in preference to laurel.12

Two reviews in periodicals with a religious orienta-
tion took a rather different point of view. Roswell P.
Barnes summarized the action of Jack Kelso and then asserted that Masters had asked some tremendously significant
and provocative questions in his poem. The poet had inveighed against the abuses in our political and economic sys-
tem, the atrocities in our industrial order, and monstrosi-
ties in our social and religious customs. Unfortunately he
did not offer any answers to his questions. 13 An anonymous
review in the Christian Century asserted that Masters's device of using a minor character as a medium for criticizing
trends in the national life was successful and insisted that
the poet's indictment of American civilization, while not always confirmed, was intelligently drawn. Masters had something to say and was clearly worth listening to. Both reviews stressed the philosophical substance of Jack Kelso
rather than the story or the form, although the Christian
Century reviewer did object to the lumbering movement of
the narrative and to Masters's carelessness in rhyming.14

The consensus seemed to be that Jack Kelso was a
more interesting work than Lee since the fisherman-poet was
a more viable figure than the shadowy Confederate general
and since the Illinois background was at least temporarily
clearer than the vague Virginia landscape. But neither work
was dramatically effective and both dealt with ideas more
than with characters and action. Masters's dramatic ability
was definitely suspect, a verdict which unfortunately became
even more completely confirmed when the later narratives
appeared. On the other hand, his claim to the title of poet
was often surprisingly verified by the appearance of songs
or lyric passages which had genuine beauty.

Three years after the publication of Jack Kelso Masters produced another long poem in which a minor character in the earlier narrative became the protagonist. Jack Kelso ends with the hero rescuing a lad named Godbey from a well into which he had fallen. In Godbey: A Dramatic Poem (1931), Masters presents Godbey as a middle-aged man who wanders back to the well into which he had once fallen. This time he reenters the well and meets a spirit named Euphemia with whom he tours another world which is strangely like the topsy-turvy world he has just left. Fifteen scenes or visions introduce Godbey to various places; the fool Dagonet serves as his guide. Eventually, Godbey emerges from the well and sits beside the village idiot Mc-Namar, and the poem concludes with the intimation that all of Godbey's experiences took place in a dream. To bring this artificial story to an end Masters requires almost six thousand lines of rhymed verse.

Godbey received little notice and the reviews that did appear were hostile. Eda Lou Walton began her notice by remarking that Spoon River Anthology owed part of its success to the fact that it appeared at the height of the vers libre movement and at a time when other writers such as Dreiser, Lewis, and Anderson were also exploring the sordidness of life in a small town. When Masters turned to satire he employed a medium in which he was less adept and, especially in Godbey, produced a long satirical allegory. Miss Walton complained that Godbey is not only a confused narrative which does not hold the reader's attention but that it is written in conventional verse rhythms which frequently collapse into doggerel. She also asserted that Masters was not temperamentally equipped to be a satirist. He could hate bitterly but he lacked both detachment and distance; thus his attacks on politics, religion, law, and scholarship are vehement without being convincing. Since Masters was unable to define his characters clearly he was also unable to give sharp outline to the basic issues.15 Louis Untermeyer was even more emphatic. Godbey was not only structurally dependent on a familiar and wornout device but its thousands of pedestrian couplets were largely given over to diatribe and debate. Untermeyer was willing to admit that the poem had ideas, even that occasionally there were surprisingly clear lyrics; he could not, however, get pleasure from the verse and he claimed that Masters's besetting sin was not dogmatism but dullness.16

Even while engaged in the creation of Godbey Masters

found it possible to publish another narrative poem, or rather three dramatic poems linked only by their concern with one basic theme. Gettysburg, Manila, Acoma, published in 1930, deals with the notion that the sole criterion by which one is to be judged is loftiness of purpose. Thus John Wilkes Booth and Emilio Aguinaldo, assassin and rebel, were really spiritual heroes following out what they conceived to be their own destinies, while the Indians of Acoma, superficial converts to Catholicism, were actually sun worshipers still faithful to the ancient religion. Reviewers were quick to point out that these were closet dramas with a disproportionate ratio of soliloquy to dialogue. Acoma alone seemed to have any theatrical qualities. For the most part the poems were stiffly written and the characters lacked reality.

William Rose Benét gave Masters credit for a comprehensive knowledge of American history but asserted that the blank verse frequently became tedious and even the lyrical interludes did not always avoid banality. Benét even preferred William Vaughn Moody's indictment of American imperialism to that of Masters.17 A brief notice in the New York Times Book Review contended that Masters was a man of keen intellect, sympathetic adjustments to environment, and no little poetic skill. His attempt to deal poetically with important themes merited praise, but the three works lacked impact because they contained not fully bodied characters but mere voices.18 Horace Gregory also attempted to find some basis for appreciation of the three dramatic poems. Masters's onslaught against American imperialism would be welcome to many ears, and the poet's "doctor-lawyer-small-town-atheist personality" remains an important element in American literature. But Gettysburg, Manila, Acoma was obviously Masters at his worst, or as Gregory more succinctly put it, Masters on a spree. 19

It should be observed that neither Godbey nor Gettysburg, Manila, Acoma won much recognition. Few reviews appeared and even the writers of these seemed ill at ease. Godbey was never republished and Gettysburg, Manila, Acoma was issued only in a limited edition of 375 copies. Today, copies are sparse and not easily accessible. The University of Illinois Library, for example, has neither volume in its collection of something more than five million books. The contemporary verdict that the two titles would add nothing to the reputation of Edgar Lee Masters seems to have been fully confirmed.

Of the three remaining long narrative poems that Masters published in the decade of the 1930's only one, The New World, got much attention. This curious work, set in 1934, was virtually unnoticed. Richmond, which appeared in the capital of the Confederacy during the tragic closing days of the war, tells a melodramatic domestic story against the military background. Corinne, the heroine, has had both lover and husband. Her own child dies as an infant and she is an accomplice in the murder of her husband's illegitimate child by a Negro woman. When the two men face each other, they duel, and the husband kills the lover, only to be fatally stabbed by Corinne. At the end the wife speaks a choral lament with the conscious recognition that she is a symbol of the ruined South and the destruction of liberty. Despite the violent action the speeches are long and rhetorical, and any dramatic action subsides under a flood of rhetoric. Richmond, a thin volume of fifty-five pages, was published by Samuel French in New York and Los Angeles rather than by Masters's usual publisher, Macmillan.

The Golden Fleece of California was issued in a signed edition of 550 copies by the Countryman Press of Weston, Vermont, in 1936 and also in the same year by Farrar and Rinehart. It received at least two reviews, neither very enthusiastic.

Eda Lou Walton thought that the basic idea of the poem was attractive. The California Gold Rush continued to interest readers and the argonaut story was inherently dramatic. But she claimed that the narrative movement was unfortunately slow and impeded furthermore by bits of mystical philosophy, all of which obscured the real thrust of the poem. Masters's work once again suffered the more he departed from the realistic material of his early writing and the more he withdrew from his pure studies of American people and culture. Thus The Golden Fleece of California became a little pompous, with the symbols often clearly forced.[20]

Burroughs Mitchell, writing in the Nation, devoted some space to the argument of the poem. Masters began his story with the departure of a small band of students from McKendree College, Illinois, in 1848 for the California gold fields. They were no more successful than most of the seekers; of the five men and one woman who leave the Middle West with high hopes, only three reach their destination. One man drowns en route, two die of cholera, and the precious gold metal eludes them all. California gold exacts as severe a toll as the legendary golden fleece of Colchis, and the moral that Masters drew at the end of his didactic poem is unfortunately heavy.

Mitchell's review emphasizes the links between Masters's use of American history and his knowledge of the classic argonauts. To many readers the quest for California gold is an exciting story, often full of harrowing details. Yet Masters proved unable to translate his narrative into successful verse. As the critic put it, "The verse is slovenly, wavering between labored attempts at dignity and informal chatter, and the many opportunities for drama and tension are entirely missed." Once again Masters, in his eagerness to rush into print, was guilty of clumsy writing which often reduced his poetry to something little better than an uninspired dog trot.21

A brief and scornful notice was contributed by Evelyn Scott to Poetry. To her The Golden Fleece of California was cinematograph poetry, apparently intended for the adolescent mind of the movie public. Masters, a familiar and well established writer, was spiritually immature. His poem never glowed sensuously, and on the intellectual level completely lacked significance.22

Similar criticism was directed by various reviewers at The New World, the long narrative poem which Masters published in 1937, although generally readers were impressed by the scope of the poem and by the flood of ideas developed in it. A panoramic view of American history since the days of the early Viking incursions into North America, The New World is both a chronicle and an indictment. The poem lacks a central figure and a core episode; it is a pageant rather than a dramatic story. But Masters's intensity and bitterness, directed against the greed for gold that several centuries of American history reveal, provide an interest which otherwise would be lacking.

To Kerker Quinn in the New York Herald Tribune Books Masters completely disregarded dramatic scenes or characterization.23 He was apparently interested chiefly in the evils of so-called civilization on the North American continent, and as a result produced what could only be called a moralist's diatribe against American materialism. But oddly enough, as the poem progressed it actually improved stylistically, proof perhaps that on occasion one of God's truly angry men could write eloquently.

Time, in one of its typically caustic and flippant reviews, asserted that Masters had produced nothing of significance since 1915 and that the thirty-two volumes of humdrum prose and verse that he had published after Spoon River Anthology had disappointed his most loyal public. The review labeled The New World as Disappointment No. 33. According to the critic, Masters presented a detailed catalogue of the slips whereby the New World failed to achieve its original promise. One was the Civil War (as the poet said, "No good came out of it that would not have come without it."). This was followed by the age of gas, initiated by that "logo-lyrist" Woodrow Wilson, and the age of soap grease sponsored by Franklin D. Roosevelt. The latest slip was the relegation of the Constitution to the scrapheap. The only merit that the Time reviewer could find in The New World was the author's earnestness and honesty.[24]

Harold Rosenberg, in a short review in Poetry, approved of Masters's heated attack on imperialism but thought that prose would have served for this purpose better than verse. Rosenberg actually said little about language or style. Louis Untermeyer, on the other hand, was scornful. He pointed out that in 1938 Masters was simply the victim of the demon of productivity--no less than six books in two years. He conceded that at least two of the volumes, the biographies of Whitman and Vachel Lindsay, were meritorious and full of arresting ideas, but that they as well as the poetry suffered from lamentable lapses in style. The New World, in sharp contrast to the concision of Spoon River Anthology, was blurred in outline and tiresome even to a dogged reader. Masters had not only attempted too much but had once more permitted rough and careless verse to be published. Untermeyer's concluding sentence is emphatic: "The author of the most condensed portrait-epitaphs of our time has written one of the most long-winded books of our day."[25]

Curiously enough, one of the most appreciative reviews of The New World appeared in the London Times Literary Supplement. The anonymous critic called the book Masters's most ambitious poem, a long chronicle of American history from a specific point of view with much analysis of historical figures but no direct delineation. Washington, Hamilton, and Jefferson were given special attention, but Emerson received Masters's accolade as the rarest spirit produced by the New World. Like other reviews the English notice emphasized Masters's one-sided version of history: to him the Civil War was chiefly a contest of oil versus cotton, and the overall history of America was one long quest for gold. Stylistically the poem was undistinguished, written "in irregular unrhymed verse of which the lines are often only cut-up prose." The critic observed acutely that the poem had no hero, no protagonist; the focus was rather on the people, the anonymous builders and workers who had made America. In other words, The New World was Masters's version, but so unlike it in other ways, of Sandburg's The People, Yes. 26

Eight years after the publication of The New World Padraic Colum wrote a long letter to the editor of the Saturday Review of Literature in which he decried the apathy with which critics and readers had responded to the poem. 27 He thought that the appearance of the book was badly timed; a few years earlier or later would have made a difference. At any rate Colum claimed that The New World deserved attention. Its blank verse had real forensic eloquence, and Masters's mystical vision of America was effectively expressed. Colum praised Masters's long poem for its tone: "it has the tone of a man testifying." Moreover, the poet demonstrated in The New World that "the power of ideas is the real power in history." But even Colum's belated praise did little to resuscitate interest. And after The New World Masters published no more long narrative poems.

Notes

1. Independent (December 11, 1926), 117: 684-685.

2. New Republic (November 17, 1926), 48: 383.

3. Nation (January 12, 1927), 124: 45.

4. Mark Van Doren, "The Liberty of General Lee," New York Herald Tribune Books (October 10, 1926), 7.

5. ELM, Jack Kelso (New York and London, 1928), 151.

6. John T. Frederick, "Mr. Masters Scolds," New York Herald Tribune Books (August 12, 1928), 3-4.

7. J. Dana Tasker, "History After a Fashion," Outlook

(July 25, 1928), 149: 515.

8. _Dial_ (November, 1928), 85: 442.

9. Llewellyn Jones, "Lincoln's Country," _Saturday Review of Literature_ (October 6, 1928), 5: 182.

10. H[arriet] M[onroe], _Poetry: A Magazine of Verse_ (June, 1929), 34: 177.

11. Leon Whipple, "Poets Americano," _Survey_ (November 1, 1928), 61: 169.

12. John Carter, "Mr. Masters Lingers On in the Graveyard," _New York Times Book Review_ (July 1, 1928), 5.

13. Roswell P. Barnes, "Jack Kelso," _World Tomorrow_ (October, 1928), 11: 424.

14. "Books in Brief," _Christian Century_ (August 9, 1928), 45: 979.

15. Eda Lou Walton, "Masters as Satirist," _New York Herald Tribune Books_ (December 27, 1931), 4.

16. Louis Untermeyer, "Et Praeterea Nihil," _Saturday Review of Literature_ (December 26, 1931), 8: 412.

17. William Rose Benét, "Round About Parnassus," _Saturday Review of Literature_ (July 5, 1930), 6: 1176.

18. _New York Times Book Review_ (July 27, 1930), 10. Review signed P. H.

19. Horace Gregory, "Mr. Masters on a Spree," _Nation_ (August 27, 1930), 131: 226-227.

20. Eda Lou Walton, "A Poem by Edgar Lee Masters," _New York Times Book Review_ (November 16, 1936), 39.

21. Burroughs Mitchell, _Nation_ (May 1, 1937), 144: 516.

22. Evelyn Scott, "The Test of Maturity," _Poetry: A Magazine of Verse_ (July, 1937), 50: 215-219.

23. Kerker Quinn, "A Historical Narrative," New York Herald Tribune Books (November 21, 1937), 23.

24. "Old Man Spoon River," Time (November 22, 1937), 30: 80-81, No. 21.

25. Harold Rosenberg, "Two Tales," Poetry: A Magazine of Verse (January, 1938), 51: 213-215; L[ouis] U[ntermeyer], "Poetry," Saturday Review of Literature (January 1, 1938), 17: 21, No. 10.

26. "Epic of America," London Times Literary Supplement (January 1, 1938), No. 1874, 8.

27. Padraic Colum, "Masters's The New World," Saturday Review of Literature (March 24, 1945), 28: 15, 32.

CHAPTER 7

FICTION

Contemporary readers attracted to the literary work
of Edgar Lee Masters think of him as a writer of poetry
and biography, the fields in which his fame was most durable. They do not remember him as a writer of fiction.
Indeed, it is rather unusual for a man who has devoted the
greater part of his creative life to poetry to turn his attention to the novel, even briefly. One remembers, of course,
that Sir Walter Scott had a career as a narrative poet before producing the Waverley Novels, that Thomas Hardy was
almost equally renowned as poet and novelist, that Oliver
Wendell Holmes wrote <u>Elsie Venner</u> as well as his amusing
vers de société, that <u>Stephen Crane</u> produced memorable
verse as well as <u>The Red Badge of Courage</u>. In our own
day, William Carlos Williams wrote a good many short stories, Carl Sandburg was the author of one long novel, Re-
membrance <u>Rock</u>, and James Dickey probably has achieved
as much recognition for his story <u>Deliverance</u> as for his poetry. It remains true, nevertheless, that writers do not
generally achieve equal recognition for poetry and for prose
fiction, even when narrative seems to be their particular interest. Poetic qualities such as concision, paradox, rhyme,
and a regular rhythm do not always confer distinction on imaginative prose narrative.

Between 1920 and 1937 Masters published seven novels. The manuscripts in the University of Texas collection
also include the scripts of short stories written at various
times. Since Masters always showed a strong compulsion
toward narrative writing and since his gift for portraiture
appeared in some of his earliest publications, it is obvious
that he adopted any literary form which would expose his
storytelling ability to the public. Previous chapters have already emphasized the views of many critics that much of

Masters's narrative poetry might have been more effective if couched in prose. Masters also undoubtedly hoped that prose fiction would secure a vastly larger audience for him, a goal which he did not achieve. It is well to note that he actually turned to the novel rather late in life. He was fifty-two years of age when he published his first novel, sixty-nine when his last appeared in 1937. His final novel was his longest and his most ambitious work of prose fiction.

Although Masters's novels were widely reviewed when they first appeared, they have since attracted little attention. Only one article has been published which surveys his fictional accomplishment as a whole, John T. Flanagan's essay "The Novels of Edgar Lee Masters" in the South Atlantic Quarterly.1 Perhaps most surprising is that Masters's novels are scarcely mentioned in histories of American fiction. There are no textual discussions and no index references to Masters's novels in either Arthur Hobson Quinn's American Fiction of 1936 or Alexander Cowie's The Rise of the American Novel of 1948. Edward Wagenknecht also ignored Masters in his Cavalcade of the American Novel (1952). Even in two studies of literary genres Masters got short shrift. Ernest E. Leisy, in The American Historical Novel (1950), cites two of the novels in a kind of briefly annotated chronological survey in an appendix; and Harry Bernard, in Le Roman régionaliste aux Etats-Unis (1949), provides a brief discussion of one novel, Mitch Miller. Masters fared no better in two surveys of American fiction published in the middle 1930's. Harlan Hatcher's Creating the Modern American Novel (1935) cited Spoon River Anthology three times but ignored the novels; Harry Hartwick's The Foreground of American Fiction (1934), listed The Nuptial Flight among novels concerned with marriage and divorce and observed that in Mitch Miller, Skeeters Kirby, and Kit O'Brien Masters "exposed the rancid, falsely respectable town of Petersburg, Illinois."2 One can only conclude that Masters's novels have left no great impression on the critics and historians of American fiction. But contemporary reviewers sometimes reached a very different verdict.

All of Masters's seven novels deal with Illinois, generally with rural or small town Illinois but with a few scenes located in Chicago. Petersburg, Masters's boyhood home, appears under its own name; elsewhere Masters invents towns such as Whitehall and Ferrisburg. But certainly the shadow of Spoon River rests on all the communities.

Four of the novels--Mitch Miller, Skeeters Kirby, Kit O'-Brien, and Mirage--clearly derive from the Spoon and Sangamon valleys and Masters's youthful experiences there. Indeed, autobiographical material is rich in this group, and Masters himself, his father, and his paternal grandparents appear, often under thin disguises. The other major influence was Mark Twain, whose themes and methods the writer almost consciously imitated. Readers who remember with pleasure the exploits of Huck Finn and Tom Sawyer will recognize the models here, even though the Illinois and Hannibal is transmuted into Petersburg. As one critic pointed out, "The narrator of Mitch Miller is Skeeters Kirby, who plays Huck Finn to Mitch's Tom Sawyer and later Horatio to the more literate boy's Hamlet."3 Masters even used the narrative form employed so effectively by Twain. These novels are first-person stories, and to a large extent Skeeters Kirby and Kit O'Brien speak the simple, colloquial, often illiterate language of small town adolescents.

The other three novels are historical chronicles, written more objectively and having at times an epic sweep as they attempt to document the history of Illinois throughout much of the nineteenth century. Children of the Market Place tells a fictional story but makes a hero out of Stephen A. Douglas. The Nuptial Flight delineates three successive marriages and shows the family's moral degeneration from the arrival of the pioneers to the early maturity of the grandson. The Tide of Time is an opulent documentary of an Illinois small town which is closely and continuously related to the career of a Jeffersonian idealist. All three novels, utilizing the third person point of view, permitted Masters to air his views on American history and politics as the nineteenth century unrolled before him. Too often, as various critics perceived at once, the exposition got in the way of the narrative; but the novelist's skill in portraiture and storytelling won him for the moment a fairly wide audience.

Charles C. Baldwin, in an early interview with Masters, recorded some interesting comments which the writer made about his first novel, Mitch Miller (1920). Masters admitted that he had used the names of real places, such as Petersburg, Havana, Springfield, Bobtown, Oakford, and Atterberry, and that in some instances he had introduced the names of actual persons.

I have also drawn upon the knowledge that I have of this part of Illinois and its people as they were when I lived there as a boy. My attempt has been to portray these people, the country and the events used in utmost fidelity and to put into them the feelings of a boy, the knowledge and understanding of a boy, perhaps somewhat emphasized, but through the method of quotation from older people who spoke in the presence of these boys and whose words impressed them.4

In other words, Masters strove as far as it was possible to make his fiction authentic.

The resemblance of Mitch Miller to Huckleberry Finn disturbed some reviewers although they generally found merit in the book. Marguerite Fellows in Publishers' Weekly called the work "a poignant little story, tragic in parts, but never morbid." She added that in this Middle Western idyll of boy life in the shadow of the Civil War, Lincoln and Tom Sawyer seemed almost equally real to the lads seeking adventure in the Illinois Valley. Her final remark was often echoed in subsequent reviews: Masters had written here a book for both boys and adults. A similarly brief notice in the Outlook called Mitch Miller both unusual and captivating, with the implication that more mature readers would respond to it because of the subtlety shown by Masters in his depiction of Mitch's temperament.5

One of the earliest important reviews appeared in the New York Times Book Review.6 The critic made the familiar comment that Masters had never equalled Spoon River Anthology but expressed so much interest in Mitch Miller, despite some obvious flaws, that he advised the author to let poetry rest and devote his time to fiction. Mitch Miller, he observed, began as a boy's book, but after Mitch and Skeeters learned that Tom Sawyer had never existed, the tone changed sharply and the novel became virtually a commentary on life and fate. Most readers would probably be shocked by Mitch's early death, the result of an accidental injury suffered when the boy tried to hitch a ride on a freight train. On the other hand, Masters accounted for the event plausibly. The visit to Hannibal disillusioned Mitch and he was further frustrated by his rejected devotion to Zueline. If Mitch had become the poet that he envisioned, he would have been a bitter one. The reviewer found the first three-quarters of the novel delightful, a meticulous account of boy life supposedly written by Skeeters Kirby, with an absorbing treasure hunt and courtroom scene. Later the novel quite obviously became a psychological study designed for adults. The conclusion of the review must have both pleased and annoyed Masters: the suggestion, namely, that he should continue with fiction and let poetry rest for a long time.

Carl Van Doren thought that the novel contained too much elegy and argument to interest boys and argued that the plot was needlessly tangled and cumbersome. He conceded that Mitch Miller had touches of comedy, bits of excellent portraiture, and even some racy prose, but claimed that none of these elements appeared often enough to give the book genuine significance."7 A review in the Freeman, however, was highly enthusiastic. Masters, according to the critic, was not here a cynic as in Spoon River Anthology but actually a poet. Mitch Miller was a lively and amusing picture of youth and, with its breadth of interpretation and singleness of mood, came close to being a masterpiece. 8 On the other hand, Edmund Lester Pearson admitted that Mitch Miller had interesting material but objected to the injection of politics. He asserted that Mark Twain could write about the 1850 period in 1874-1884 with remarkable success, whereas Masters writing about 1884-1888 could never forget 1920. Oddly enough, Pearson remarked that a perusal of Mitch Miller actually sent him back to Spoon River Anthology which he reread for the tenth time. 9 Harry Bernard, writing about American regional literature for a Canadian French audience, gave a sympathetic account of the book but labelled it "Roman de l'enfance américaine, dans un Illinois disparu."10

An English review of Mitch Miller was moderately enthusiastic. The writer thought that Masters's novel, obviously descended from Tom Sawyer, lacked some of the humor and pathos of its predecessor but had merits of its own. "Carrying one away to Abraham Lincoln's home-village, amid the human hayseed antiques of American back-town life, its quietude brings refreshment and relief after the storm, struggle, force and shouting vanities of London or New York. 11

Mitch Miller's story in the novel of which he is the title character is told by Skeeters Kirby. In 1923 Masters continued the narrator's own story in the book entitled Skeeters Kirby. Reviewers in general accepted it as a natural continuation and perceived strong autobiographical elements in it. One reviewer thought that Masters was more successful as novelist than as poet because "he is handicapped by none of the technical obstacles of a vehicle he has not completely mastered."12 With prose as a medium Masters could avoid the wooden diction which often cramped his blank verse, and since he generally dealt with the prosaic facts of life his style was obviously more appropriate. A review of the plot underscored striking similarities between Skeeters Kirby and the novelist himself: a rural childhood, village life, study of the law urged by his father, the departure for Chicago, and many love affairs, all productive of a sense of failure or futility but nevertheless leaving Skeeters resolute in his determination to fight toward a goal. The critic asserted that the protagonist-narrator was admirably characterized although not always presented as attractive, and called the novel "a noteworthy contribution to present-day American realism."

A brief notice in the Dial called the novel Masters's attempt to portray the artist as a young man. Skeeters Kirby was described as a garrulous and uneven piece of work which nevertheless showed a sensitive use of its material and fitfully able execution.13 Another anonymous review asserted that the protagonist was essentially a rebel against his environment. Skeeters always strove to dominate and was invariably defeated. Beauty eluded him, deep spiritual experience resisted his efforts to plumb it, and his aspirations dissolved into sordid realities. The critic's chief complaint, however, was that Masters was fundamentally more a social commentator than a novelist. Sinclair Lewis could write humorously about the faults of contemporary society and still inject zest into his narrative. Masters was passionately serious but undeniably powerful in his accumulation of hard, unlovely details.14

John W. Crawford's review in the Nation summarized the chief events of Skeeters Kirby's life as the narrator enumerated them, and observed the prominence of emotional affairs even though the novel closes when Kirby is only thirty-three. Six romances from adolescence to maturity enable Masters to comment on seductions of various kinds, free love, the inanities of the rich, and divorce. The character is surprisingly like the novelist: both grow up in a village, study literature and philosophy despite paternal and local opposition, proceed through a snarl of broken friendships, and find solace only in the wisdom of another generation. As Crawford put it, "Kirby has faith in his grandmother and relates his problems and difficulties to her serenity as to the one large absolute of his life."15

Johan J. Smertenko commended Skeeters Kirby as a significant novel which dealt successfully with the whole life of man. Masters here revealed Kirby in relation to sweetheart and prostitute, to an unloved betrothed and a too dear mistress; but "there are also work and study, friends and family, struggles and riches, dreams and achievements." Somewhat surprisingly, Smertenko saw in the novel not only a full-length human portrait but also the "completest study we have of the contemporary artist from the Middle West." Masters, he thought, had achieved a kind of composite portrait of Dreiser, Anderson, Dell, and Lewis! The critic was not unaware of certain imperfections, however, and complained about the jejune prose and the lack of humor. But he praised Masters for his ability at characterization.16

The Skeeters Kirby story continues into a third novel, Mirage, which appeared in 1924. In a long review in the New Republic Robert Herrick commented on the earlier books as well as the story under immediate consideration.17 Herrick, a Chicago novelist who had written a series of novels dealing with social and professional life, was well qualified to review Masters's fiction although he was not generally sympathetic. He pointed out that when Masters turned to prose in such novels as Mitch Miller and Skeeters Kirby, "he revived in a tender, reminiscential mood the associations of his earlier years, with their homely, intimate quite American background." Mitch Miller was notably successful for its limpid style and boy-like fancifulness. But Mirage, in Herrick's view, exemplified the worst style that Masters had written in verse or prose. It not only lacked the restraint and vigor which he had previously shown, but it was actually banal and flat. Herrick also disliked what he called the sexual promiscuity of the novel. He discounted Masters's reputation as a realist, claiming that Kirby's affair with Becky Norris (Kirby's Circe) had neither credibility nor significance. Herrick contended that a Circe, to be successful, must possess both subtlety and power; not only did Becky Norris lack both, but her victim was equally wanting in spiritual distinction.

H. W. Boynton considered Mirage with other contemporary novels and found little to distinguish it. He claimed that Masters's novels did no more than develop in bulk and detail the life stories that the famous Spoon River Anthology had compressed into a dozen lines. Skeeters Kirby, again the protagonist, resembled other fictional figures in being essentially ineffectual and even pathetic. "His resentment is stronger than his vision: so that his net effect is egocentric and negative, not generous or positive."18

Similar remarks appeared in an anonymous notice in the Literary Review.19 The critic felt that Mirage was a muddled story of a priggish writer who wasted years in a sexual obsession with a woman whom he knew to be worthless. "It is topheavy in construction, vulgar in thought, provincial in expression, and preposterously lacking in humour." Masters invited sympathy for his protagonist and yet failed to make Kirby anything more than a frustrated writer who was doomed to defeat. As a result much of the novel was muddy in thought. The closing pages, nevertheless, proved that Masters could do better and provided some of the beauty and wisdom which the reader had missed earlier in the book.

Harry Salpeter wrote an equally critical review. He conceded that the modern novel, unlike the work of Fielding or Thackeray, could well include social satire, autobiography, muckraking, theology, and political science, all of which seemed to be represented in Mirage.20 But Masters's novel unfortunately seemed to have negligible action and to represent woman as a succubus, dank and poisonous. If the book had a thesis it was deceptively simple: marriage is a failure. Every man and woman in the story is divorced or has been unhappily married; the reader can thus conclude that Mirage is a Schopenhauerian version of the Canterbury Tales. Salpeter objected to the redundant flashbacks and recapitulations, and to the subordination of action to debate and controversy. Nor was the critic happy about Masters's prose style, though he contented himself with the remark that the novelist's sentences were not always fortunately constructed.

H. L. Mencken was almost completely denunciatory. A brief sketch in the fifth series of Prejudices praised Spoon River Anthology and admitted that Mitch Miller included some fine touches among its many banalities. But Mirage was something quite different. Mencken asserted, "It seems to me to be one of the most idiotic and yet one of the most interesting American novels that I have ever read."21 Mirage contained philosophical palaver at about the level of barbershop conversation, and characters who were stuffed dummies creaking at every joint; yet Masters also introduced shrewd and gracefully phrased observations plus some people who were as alive as those of Dreiser and Willa Cather. Mencken quoted a long dialogue passage spoken by Skeeters Kirby and Becky Norris to represent his charge of inconceivable banality, and accused the novel of triteness, stiltedness, and a naive lack of humor. In comparison with the heroic and lovely lines of the Anne Rutledge epitaph, Mirage seemed a disaster.

With most of these complaints Ludwig Lewisohn disagreed. In his Nation review of Mirage he observed that while Masters had the full equipment of the novelist, including the ability to characterize and to dramatize action, he had really written here largely as a poet. Moreover, Masters had succeeded in creating plausible people. Becky Norris, whom Herrick had dismissed as an unsuccessful Circe, Lewisohn called a "magnificent full-length portrait of an utterly detestable woman." Becky was a liar, a parasite, an egoist, but still an overwhelmingly true-to-life person. Masters was not necessarily a misogynist in delineating such a woman; his story was rather an invective and a warning. Skeeters Kirby indeed inhabited a sorry social world which drove him into a moody philosophic nihilism, but Lewisohn did not impugn Masters's credibility in describing it.[22]

Masters's fourth novel to use Sangamon Valley material was Kit O'Brien (1927). In an introductory note he stated that he deliberately chose Petersburg as the locale of the story because it grew out of Mitch Miller, but he warned his readers not to insist on too literal a reading, and declared that he was really concerned with the American small town in general. He added, "I love that town of my boyhood, its people and its ways too deeply to dispraise them, or to say anything but good of them." Again he had his protagonist tell the story in the first person and use the colloquial diction of boyhood. As Kit says, "Parents is like freckles or cross eyes or anythin': you jest have 'em; but because you do it's no sign that you ought to."[23] The quality of the novel was well expressed by a note in the Booklist: "This story of a mid-western boyhood, told in the boy's own language, is as much a social document as a novel, for in it are depicted the strata of life in a small town, the ways of social and civil justice."[24]

Reviewers expressed little enthusiasm about Kit O'Brien but on the whole found little to object to. A critic

for the Saturday Review of Literature called it, like Huckleberry Finn, a simple, effective story with strong documentary value, a book about boys which was probably intended
for nature readers. A reviewer for the New York Times
Book Review echoed this opinion but remarked that the theft
of a pie, which precipitated Kit's flight from Petersburg and
started his adventures, hardly seemed a great event in the
annals of crime. Kit himself, nevertheless, seemed quite
convincing.[25]

One of the longest reviews, although devoted largely
to plot summary, was the work of Llewellyn Jones.[26] He
felt that Masters had filled the book with conventional and
social criticism: there was an unjust district attorney,
plutocrats ran the village of Petersburg for their own ag-
grandizement, and too often there were fights between capitalized Right and Wrong. Yet Jones remarked that the book
was a pleasing gesture from an author known for his icono-
clasm.

The three historical novels that Masters published between 1922 and 1937 are much less autobiographical, have
little to do with the Sangamon Valley of his boyhood, although they picture Illinois at various historical times, and
often tend to become a platform from which he can dissemi-
nate his views on politics and society. Missing completely
are the charm and intimacy of Masters's stories of boyhood,
while the documentation is often heavy and tends to increase
his natural prolixity. Nevertheless, more than one reviewer found strong merits in these fictions even when, like
Henry Seidel Canby, they thought that Masters might better
have written straight biography.

Children of the Market Place (1922) introduces a fictional hero, James Miles, who comes to America to learn
about his father's estate and discovers that he has a mulatto
half sister. James Miles has his own unexciting adventures
but it is chiefly through his eyes that we see Stephen A.
Douglas, the political figure with whom Masters was in
closest sympathy. Douglas becomes the dominant character
in the book. In her Survey review Florence Fleisher carefully refrained from making any literary judgment but pointed out that Masters's historical novel about the economic
forces affecting American expansionism was really an analysis of the present in the light of the past. She felt that in
this limited way the novelist had produced an admirable
piece of work but that his story was inconsequential.[27]

H. W. Boynton in the Independent dealt largely with Masters's handling of slavery and moral problems and emphasized Douglas's conviction that ethics was of less importance than states' rights in settling controversial questions. Boynton also said little about Children of the Market Place as a fictional narrative.[28] A third brief review in the Outlook was almost equally noncommittal about aesthetic qualities. But the critic observed that Douglas was clearly presented as the central figure and that the reader got almost a spectator's view of the slavery agitation and of the development of transportation via canal boat, stage coach, and railroad. He added that the book was "remarkable as a study of American life and of the conflict of race and political passions in the period treated."[29]

The Dial review was generally negative. The critic remarked that the novel "which elbows its way through Mr. Masters's historical lumber is curiously devoid of human interest." The characters seemed placidly dead despite Masters's earlier proof that he could draw character, and the style, although sometimes galvanic, was not always grammatical. Probably the author made his greatest mistake in trying to produce a history and a novel simultaneously.[30]

Austin Hay in the New York Times Book Review considered Children of the Market Place ostensibly a work of fiction but actually "an admirable piece of historical interpretation." Hay approved of the framework Masters had chosen for his story since it enabled the writer to give an excellent analysis of Douglas. The Little Giant's views of manifest destiny and of popular sovereignty were clearly set forth. Masters believed that the Democrats, in failing to nominate Douglas for the presidency on a united ticket, lost their chance to defeat Lincoln and thus avoid a fratricidal war. But in Masters's view, Douglas was not a failure but indeed as much of an empire builder as Cecil Rhodes. His only real flaw was a basic materialism. The reviewer claimed that Children of the Market Place was a skillful blending of diverse elements and was written in an agreeable flowing style. He concluded that the novel was "one of the most delightful and yet thoughtful contributions to the storehouse of contemporary American literature."[31]

Henry Seidel Canby's review of the novel was probably the most sympathetic of all. The editor of the Literary Review did not welcome the technique which Masters employed since he felt that the James Miles story got in the way of the Douglas chronicle, which after all was the real raison d'etre of the book. To be sure, Miles as a subordinate character could act as the medium of comment on the great events of the time, but he detracted from Douglas, and the portrait of the Little Giant gave life and force to the novel. To Canby, Children of the Market Place was a superior political novel, a story which proved readable, interesting, and informative. But he had one striking reservation. He wondered why Masters chose to use the Douglas theme for fiction at all when straight biography seemed to be closer to Masters's real metier. Whether or not Masters read this review, it is interesting to remember that in the next dozen years he produced no less than four important biographies--of Lincoln, Vachel Lindsay, Whitman, and Mark Twain.32

The Nuptial Flight (1923) is a panoramic view of Illinois small town life as a background for the story of three marriages. Emigrants from Kentucky arrive at Whitehall in 1849. The pioneers, William and Nancy Houghton, work hard and establish themselves in the new community. They become universally admired and loved octogenarians, very much like Masters's own paternal grandparents. Their children and grandchildren, however, are less successful and certainly less happy. Walter Scott Houghton, handsome and spoiled, fails at most of his occupations and is not helped by his selfish, nagging, and irascible wife Fanny. His son Alfred becomes a violinist and marries a considerably older woman who has scant sympathy for his professional ambitions and little regard for his social well being. Thus the nuptial flight has turned out badly for most of the free souls who try it.

Malcolm Cowley, who took the usual view that Masters had never equalled Spoon River Anthology, thought that The Nuptial Flight was superior to most of the later verse and preferred it to the other novels. But he admitted no enthusiasm about it. With the exclusion of Fanny Houghton, a vivid portrait of a completely malicious and lazy person, Cowley claimed that the characters were dull and mechanically revealed. He suggested oddly enough that Masters's own adventures since the appearance of the famous epitaphs would have been a more interesting story. He also criticized the writer for a prosaic, journalistic style which did not help the readability of the novel.33

The New York Times Book Review printed a bitterly

negative review.[34] The anonymous critic asserted that the novel would never have been noticed at all except for the fact that it was the work of the author of Spoon River Anthology. Masters had already proved that he was capable of writing an effective picture of Middle Western life but he had subsequently been working too hard or thinking too hard. Unfortunately, his thoughts were naive. Masters had learned three things: love is a biological force which brings both delight and trouble; the human race has two basic catetories, the eaters and the creators; and the faulty divorce and alimony laws of the United States give the eater a good deal of help. The characters in this unsuccessful novel were dull and stupid. American divorce procedure was certainly in need of reform but changes could hardly be brought about by a novel so incoherent "that its characters seem to need a lunacy commission rather than a court of domestic relations."

A completely contrary point of view was expressed by Ludwig Lewisohn, who was so impressed by The Nuptial Flight that he asserted that it placed the author in the front rank of American novelists. He even expressed his hope that Masters would henceforth devote his full energy to fiction. Lewisohn found the book as rich, as deep, and as concrete as the Illinois soil which the pioneers farmed. The three-generation story impressed him and the people were vitally portrayed, especially the wives of the son and grandson, unattractive as they were. Even though the style was not always felicitous, "the narrative has a rude, quiet vigor, a patriarchal breadth and solidity."[33]

Masters's final novel, The Tide of Time, appeared in 1937. This sprawling story of 682 pages traced the history of Ferrisburg, Illinois, from about 1822 into the early twentieth century. The central character, Leonard Westerfield Atterberry, is a lawyer, congressman, and judge, a small town liberal who fought the Republican establishment in every way but seemed generally associated with losing causes. Atterberry, in many ways quite like the novelist's own father, Hardin Masters, was attractive, tolerant, and intelligent, yet was consistently opposed by the small town capitalists who did not like to see their control of the community threatened. Most reviewers appreciated Atterberry as a character but deplored the loose structure of the novel and criticized Masters's insertion of long passages about national politics which seemed almost irrelevant. And again they assailed him for careless writing. But the consensus was that at the age of sixty-nine Masters had produced not only his most ambitious but his best novel.

The _Time_ notice was succinct: Masters had tried to show how "good human material can be swept by the tide of time into shallows and onto shoals."[36] Mason Wade, in the _Nation_, accepted this point of view and described Atterberry as a Jeffersonian natural aristocrat whose liberalism came into conflict with the stubborn mediocrity of Illinois village life and whose promise was defeated by his environment.[37] Wade perceived that Masters meant to use his story of a country lawyer as a symbol of American history but claimed that the task was too much for the novelist. Only a few vivid passages redeemed the book's general tonelessness, and the frequent attempts to link small lives with great events proved generally inept. Wade concluded that careless writing and a flood of irrelevant detail spoiled an ambitious book. On the other hand, Frederick Graham believed that in this novel Masters had presented an accurate cross-section of one phase of our national heterogeneity and had filled his book with viable people. Graham observed that the characters, even if reminiscent of Spoon River, were "finely and clearly drawn with exact brush strokes," and that through the various members of the Atterberry family Masters was able to show the developing social consciousness of a representative American community. The critic admitted that too much bulky and non-essential material had been included but expressed the unusual judgment that the prose was inescapably poetic; indeed for him The Tide of Time was Masters's "outstanding prose effort."[38]

H. W. Boynton was less enthusiastic but not unfavorable. He felt that younger writers had far exceeded Masters in frankness and that his mournful, reluctant scepticism had become rather pallid.[39] Yet he called the book a storehouse. Kerker Quinn, in a long review which was little more than plot summary, remarked that as a social historian Masters was comprehensive and authoritative, while as a moralist he was vigorous; it was only as an artist striving to use fiction as his medium that he failed.[40] Probably the most perspicacious critic was Howard Mumford Jones. He saw the novel as Masters's attempt to combine the fictional biography of an Illinois town with a sketchy history of the United States after the Black Hawk War. Masters had an excellent command of Middle Western material and a feeling for the sweep of American history; however, he wrote stodgy narrative and employed a lumbering style which could be compared only with Theodore Dreiser's. His protagonist, Leonard Atterberry, was solid enough and not too unlike Clarence Darrow; but the regiment of minor figures in Jones's view were seldom more than sketches. On the whole, Jones preferred Masters's earlier boys' stories, possibly because they were more autobiographical and hence more realistic.[41]

Perhaps at this point one collective judgment of Masters's fiction needs to be cited, slight as it obviously is. In her comprehensive study of the small town in American literature Ima Herron paid some attention to the novels, particularly to Mitch Miller, which she found noticeably similar to Mark Twain's work although with an interest of its own.[42] But she barely mentioned the later books and ignored The Tide of Time. Miss Herron's chief interest in Masters was of course Spoon River Anthology which has been discussed in a previous chapter.

On balance it must be admitted that Masters did not write distinguished fiction. Prose perhaps gave him too much latitude and encouraged his natural tendency toward prolixity, while his aversion to careful revision permitted serious structural and stylistic flaws. When he chose to deal with nineteenth century American history, despite a distinct Jeffersonian bias, he was on solid ground, although he allowed his historical novels to become an arena for a protracted discussion of politics. Yet he could tell a story, he could occasionally invent memorable characters, and he could through experience and study offer a panoramic view of a region over a long period. In Masters' novels the fictional Ferrisburg, the actual Petersburg, and the composite Spoon River join the small towns of American literature.

Notes

1. John T. Flanagan, "The Novels of Edgar Lee Masters," South Atlantic Quarterly (January, 1950), 49: 82-95.

2. Harry Hartwick, The Foreground of American Fiction (New York & Cincinnati, 1934), 258.

3. Flanagan, op. cit., 84.

4. Charles C. Baldwin, The Men Who Make Our Novels

(Freeport, N.Y., 1967), 356-357. Originally published, 1924.

5. Marguerite Fellows, Publishers' Weekly (October 16, 1920), 98: 1192; Outlook (December 1, 1920), 126: 600.

6. New York Times Book Review and Magazine (November 7, 1920, 20.

7. C[arl] V[an] D[oren], Nation (November 17, 1920), 111: 566.

8. Freeman (November 10, 1920), 2: 214.

9. Edmund Lester Pearson, "New Books and Old," Weekly Review (November 10, 1920), 3: 447. This review, incidentally, also discussed Lewis's Main Street.

10. Harry Bernard, Le Roman régionaliste aux États-Unis (Montreal, 1949), 199.

11. C. E. Lawrence, (London) Bookman (August, 1921), 60: 216-217.

12. New York Times Book Review (March 4, 1923), 14, 16.

13. Dial (July, 1923), 75: 98.

14. Literary Digest International Book Review (April, 1923), 1: 53.

15. John W. Crawford, "A Pilgrim's Progress," Nation (April 18, 1923), 116: 473-474.

16. Johan J. Smertenko, "A Significant Novel," Literary Review (August 4, 1923), 3: 875-876.

17. Robert Herrick, "Mr. Masters's Prose," New Republic (June 25, 1924), 39: 138-139.

18. H. W. Boynton, "This Sorry Scheme," Outlook (May 7, 1924), 137: 31.

19. Literary Review (May 17, 1924), 4: 762.

20. Harry Salpeter, Literary Digest International Book Review (June, 1924), 2: 552.

21. H. L. Mencken, Prejudices, Fifth Series (New York, 1926), 56-63. Cf. p. 56.

22. Ludwig Lewisohn, Nation (May 28, 1924), 118: 616-617.

23. ELM, Kit O'Brien (New York, 1927), 144.

24. ALA Booklist (July, 1927), 23: 429.

25. "The Story of a Boy," Saturday Review of Literature (April 16, 1927), 3: 731; "Middle West Boyhood," New York Times Book Review (May 8, 1927), 9, 23.

26. Llewellyn Jones, "A Sentimental Holiday," New York Herald Tribune Books (April 24, 1927), 3: 7.

27. Florence Fleisher, "Prophets in Their Own Country," Survey (November 1, 1922), 49: 192, 201.

28. H. W. Boynton, "Yellow is Black," Independent (May 13, 1922), 108: 457.

29. Outlook (May 24, 1922), 131: 172.

30. Dial (October, 1922), 73: 457.

31. Austin Hay, New York Times Book Review and Magazine (July 9, 1922), 21, 28.

32. Henry Seidel Canby, "Novel or Biography?" Literary Review (May 13, 1922), 2: 651.

33. Malcolm Cowley, "Family Adventures," Literary Review (September 22, 1923), 4: 61.

34. New York Times Book Review and Magazine (August 26, 1923), 26.

35. L[udwig] L[ewisohn], "The Dance of Life," Nation (September 12, 1923), 117: 270.

36. Time (September 13, 1937), 30: 63.

Fiction

37. Mason Wade, "Spoon River Again," Nation (September 18, 1937), 145: 300-301.

38. Frederick Graham, New Republic (November 24, 1937), 93: 83.

39. H. W. Boynton, "A Novel by Edgar Lee Masters," New York Times Book Review (October 3, 1937), 6-7.

40. Kerker Quinn, New York Herald Tribune Books (September 19, 1937), 14, 18.

41. Howard Mumford Jones, "Making of the Middle West," Saturday Review of Literature (September 18, 1937), 16: 12.

42. Ima Honaker Herron, The Small Town in American Literature (Durham, 1939), 365-366.

CHAPTER 8

BIOGRAPHY

Masters early developed an interest in biography. As a high school student in Lewistown he read the accounts of great men in encyclopaedias. As a youth he heard many stories of heroes like Lincoln and U. S. Grant and Stephen A. Douglas, all conspicuous Illinois figures. In maturity he read extensively and gradually began to observe the myths, the distortions, that crept into partisan accounts of celebrities. It is unlikely that he ever accepted Emerson's dictum, "Other men are lenses through which we read our own minds." But he wrote in a magazine article in 1935 that it was highly important "that there should be understanding of a country's principal heroes. Not otherwise can a country have its true character."[1] To him Lee, Jackson, Jefferson, Poe, and Jefferson Davis were salient examples of men who had been misunderstood, even maligned, and whose careers called for reevaluation. A natural impulse thus led him to try his own hand at biography, either to narrate the stories of men he had personally known or to correct false impressions of heroes already well established in the national pantheon.

There were perhaps more specific reasons. Lives of great men certainly interested him, and in various instances he was impelled to give what he considered the true interpretation of their work and their motivation. But in two cases, the life of the Chicago lawyer Levy Mayer and the life of the Springfield poet Vachel Lindsay, the immediate availability of documents and correspondence plus the encouragement of the two widows were surely a determining factor. Furthermore, Masters always hoped for a larger audience than his books commonly secured. Prose was probably a more dependable avenue to public favor than poetry, and biography and history promised more lucrative returns than his earlier fiction had produced. Masters more than once asserted that he had turned to biography in the hope that it would be more rewarding financially.

Only one study of Masters's biographical writing has been published, Lois Hartley's "Edgar Lee Masters--Biographer and Historian."[2] This is a detailed account of the genesis and structure of the five biographies and one autobiography that Masters wrote, an account enriched by material taken from letters to Theodore Dreiser which are preserved in the Dreiser collection at the University of Pennsylvania. Miss Hartley quoted illuminatingly from the correspondence and revealed in the process some of Masters's own problems and decisions in the course of composition. Although never a careful scholar he read widely and perceptively and sometimes he was even guilty of overdocumentation. But haste, a driving compulsion to appear in print as soon as possible, was often his downfall, as more than one reviewer pointed out. According to one letter to Harriet Monroe, he read the diaries and letters of Vachel Lindsay for two months, although he made no great effort to secure all that were available to him, then wrote his book in thirty days.[3] Miss Hartley's article gives an excellent overall view of Masters's work in biography and history but it pays little attention to the reception accorded his books by reviewers and critics.

Masters's first venture into biography was written by request and was subsidized by the widow of the biographee.[4] In 1927 Masters published Levy Mayer and the New Industrial Era. His choice of subject, rather curious on the surface, can be easily explained. During Masters's law partnership with Clarence Darrow in Chicago, 1903-1911, he had business relations with another Chicago law firm. One member of the firm, Abraham Mayer, served as Masters's lawyer during his divorce suit and took care of the alimony payments and other details. In gratitude to Abraham Mayer and in return for a substantial fee Masters wrote the biography of his friend's brother, and the book was published by the Yale University Press in an edition of 1,500 copies.

It was not a happy subject for Masters and the book attracted little attention. Levy Mayer was a corporation attorney, fascinated by big business and frequently retained by the liquor interests, by Chicago meat packing companies, and even by the owners of the Iroquois Theater, which burned tragically in 1903. Masters presented the legal details of all these cases with professional adroitness but was completely out of sympathy with the fundamental philosophy of his subject. With his own background of support for the underprivileged, the underpaid waitresses and laborers, he must have experienced no little inquietude during his work on his study of a lawyer who had spent his lifetime in the employment of the plutocracy. But he filled his biography with documentation and with tributes to Levy Mayer, in general keeping his own opinions to himself. Presumably the family was satisfied.

Masters's biography of Lincoln was quite another matter. Lincoln, the Man, which appeared in 1931, was dedicated, one must assume somewhat ironically, "to the Memory of Thomas Jefferson, the preeminent philosopher-statesman of the United States, and their greatest president." The dedication clarifies the author's viewpoint; he obviously wrote as a Jeffersonian Democrat, an agrarian, a states' rightist. While probably not deliberately planned to get attention, like William Faulkner's Sanctuary, Lincoln, the Man was certainly Masters's most controversial book, definitely biased, definitely flawed, yet representative of a point of view which had some support, and not only in the South. Moreover, Masters wrote in deadly earnest, quite unconcerned about his partisanship but determined to destroy what he called the Lincoln myth. The book did not sell as well as the immediate publicity it got would suggest. Dale Warren, writing a report on the Boston book trade for the Publishers' Weekly of March 7, 1931, observed that booksellers were reluctant to stock it and patrons apparently shunned it. Warren commented that either the public was getting a little weary of biography in general or that Lincoln was a subject which must not be deprecated or maligned. No book of Masters, however, attracted so much attention in reviews, editorials, news stories, and letters to the press. Lincoln, the Man was by no means his best biography but at least temporarily it got an extraordinary amount of publicity even though it was, as the Time notice observed, the 112th biography of the martyred president.

Many of the notices were brief. The Time review, headed "Lincolnoclast," said little about the book beyond remarking that the morose author had painted Lincoln as a cold and lazy fanatic. Three passages from the book were quoted with little comment and the poem about Anne Rutledge from Spoon River Anthology was reprinted in a footnote. 5 A one-paragraph notice in the American Mercury was less critical in its implications and even complimented Masters.6 The book was obviously not for Lincoln partisans and had little new to offer to the Lincoln specialists. Masters saw Lincoln not as an idealist who preserved the Union and abolished slavery but as an ambitious opportunist who had a pernicious effect on American history. Still, the biography was an impressive piece of work even without extensive documentation. The review concluded with this sentence: "His book shows very careful preparation, and is vividly and effectively written." The Outlook notice agreed with Masters that a new life of Lincoln was overdue, since the Nicolay-Hay biography was excessively long and the Beveridge study went only to 1858. But Lincoln, the Man was badly proportioned, and even though Masters showed a keen understanding of some of the political events antecedent to the Civil War his treatment of Lincoln was more partisan than judicial.7 The Review of Reviews pointed out that Lincoln's deficiencies had never been emphasized so much in a biography and that Masters left the reader wondering how the man had ever reached the presidency. But Masters's treatment of Lincoln as a lawyer should prove of interest to the legal profession.8

Longer reviews raised other issues. William MacDonald, in the Nation, stressed the point that Masters had started out to demolish the Lincoln myth. Resting his book solidly on the facts in Beveridge's life, the biographer showed again that Lincoln was narrowly educated and not well read, that he had been a somewhat unscrupulous lawyer, and that his political career, motivated by a strong desire for office, was frequently that of a trimmer. But Masters went further and accused Lincoln of being ignorant, lazy, cold, superstitious, and undersexed. The "truth" as he saw it was actually a political diatribe, marked by violent language and intense prejudice.9

H. L. Mencken wrote a characteristically colorful review of the book. He was rather sympathetic to Masters's approach to his subject and remarked that the biographer was somewhat of an expert on American politics during the mid-century. If he presented no new facts he at least provided interesting interpretations. Mencken did not disagree with Masters's view of Lincoln as a man who by accident played an heroic role, made a preposterous and intolerable marriage, and eventually turned his back on Jacksonian tradition. Mencken contended that Lincoln, although temperamentally an agnostic, went into partnership with God and introduced sanctimoniousness into American politics. The critic generally had praise for Masters's writing, which he thought was definitely better than his work in such recent novels as Mirage, and he found the section of the book dealing with Lincoln's death and the aftermath a genuinely moving and even eloquent piece of work. Masters, in Mencken's view, was neither a Lincoln amateur nor a facile iconoclast.10

Denominational periodicals were particularly resentful of Masters's treatment of religion in his assessment of Lincoln.11 Thus the Catholic World's review was completely negative. There was, to be sure, room for a critical book on Lincoln but Masters had produced an angry, vicious, even venomous biography which had some of the peevish tone of Sinclair Lewis's Gopher Prairie descriptions. The reviewer claimed that Masters could not forgive Lincoln for being both religious and a Republican and wondered whether he hated the president more than he did God. The Christian Century review was somewhat more temperate but equally hostile.12 The critic felt that the iconoclastic book not only made the usual charges against Lincoln, of coldness in personal life, ineptness in statesmanship and craft in politics, but accused him of ultra religiosity. The biographer had allowed Lincoln only two virtues: a sense of humor and a genius at literary expression. All in all the volume would neither dim Lincoln's luster nor add to Masters's stature as biographer and historian.

Professional historians were seldom happy with the book but they tried to be objective in their assessments and often asserted the need for a reevaluation of Lincoln's career. Don C. Seitz, in a five-column review in the Bookman, did not specifically condemn the book but by selective quotation indicated his scorn for Masters's exaggerations, false interpretations, twisting of the evidence, and frank partisanship.13 Seitz thought that Masters was patently unfair in dwelling so long on Lincoln's poor white background, his illegitimate mother, his fugitive father, and his irresponsible love affairs. And he added that the biographer was simply splenetic when he criticized the great second inaugural address as the work of one "saturated with the hypocrisy of Hebraic-Puritanism." Seitz believed that Masters wrote his book to exploit the southern point of view, which certainly needed to be expressed but in a less intemperate way.

Much the same view was held by M. M. Quaife in the Mississippi Valley Historical Review.14 Quaife was hostile but tried hard to be objective. He argued that no leader, not even Lincoln, should be deified or immune to criticism. Masters was earnest in his indictment of Lincoln as a corrupter of the Constitution and a destroyer of civil liberties, but his book of eighteen chapters and 200,000 words was fundamentally a diatribe. An ardent supporter of states' rights and Jeffersonian liberalism himself, Masters presented Lincoln as a leader who allowed predatory and evil men to overthrow the government as it was established by the constitutional fathers, to subjugate sovereign states, to subvert liberties, and to leave the country helpless before the spoilers. Quaife quoted some of Masters's extreme views, such as the assertion that for seven decades the United States had had no president equal to James Monroe, and claimed that Lincoln, the Man was really the work of a prosecuting attorney, not that of an impartial judge or historian. He added an interesting final comment: if Lincoln was really responsible for all the deleterious effects and changes of his era, then Masters's book was definitely worth publication.

Claude Bowers, both a diplomat and an historian himself, did not question the facts of Masters's book since they were obviously gleaned from the respected Beveridge biography, but he wondered about the inferences drawn from them. He reviewed Masters's charges, many of which he did not deny, and commented on Lincoln's coldness and addiction to melancholia; only his sense of humor saved the president from fanaticism. Masters's last chapter, Bowers remarked, provided the clue to the book's approach. As a result of the Civil War and Lincoln's policies, the democratic republic of Thomas Jefferson and the constitutional fathers was destroyed. Bowers added that Lincoln could hardly have stopped the war-engendered forces but might have helped the South to reestablish itself earlier if he had lived. Masters's biography, he thought, was "an intensely interesting, arresting, challenging book which will create no end of bitter controversy, and have, in consequence, a wide reading."15

An interesting review appeared in the London Times Literary Supplement. Lincoln has always been a fascinating figure to English audiences and Masters's book could not fail to attract readers across the Atlantic Ocean. The reviewer observed that any critically minded study of the president would be welcome but deplored a book which was essentially a diatribe without a sense of humor. Masters set out to destroy the Lincoln myth and pictured Lincoln as the fount and origin of much of the evil in modern American life. He was not an Illinois St. Francis but a second-rate politician and a third-rate lawyer who by accident achieved the presidency. These views had some plausibility and certainly deserved exposition. But the critic felt that Masters's book was so ill-tempered and inefficient that the result was a failure.16

The most contemptuous review of Lincoln, the Man, possibly the most devastating review of a Masters work ever published in a responsible critical journal, was that contributed by Charles Willis Thompson to the New York Times Book Review.17 Thompson allowed the biography almost no virtues. Masters, he declared, was biased, partisan, inaccurate; he not only exaggerated but, oddly enough for a lawyer, he completely disregarded the evidence. Among the charges levelled at Lincoln were coldness, hypocrisy, treacherousness, and stupidity, with political craft being the worst of all. Masters admitted that Lincoln could use words felicitously but called him nevertheless a plagiarist since he got his language from the Bible. He was not even a good lawyer but was vindictive and cruel; in addition he was undersexed. Thompson pointed out that Masters did not limit his diatribe to Lincoln. He attacked the Republican party (conceived in hatred and mothered in hatred), McKinley and Hamilton, Webster and Van Buren. He even attacked some Democrats; only Stephen A. Douglas was a shining knight. Thompson's final comment was succinct: Masters had written a Copperhead biography. Neither Alexander H. Stephens nor Jefferson Davis would have produced such a study of Lincoln, but "it might have been written by an Indiana Knight of the Golden Circle."

Not many reviewers ventured to explain Masters's motivation. Perhaps Robert D. Narveson came closest to doing so in a 1961 article in which he compared the attitudes toward Lincoln expressed in poetry and prose by three Illinois writers--Sandburg, Lindsay, and Masters.18

Originally, all three had paid tribute to the president; only Masters changed his mind. He certainly had ample reason to know and admire Lincoln since he had been brought up in the New Salem-Springfield area and had spoken to men like Mentor Graham and William H. Herndon, Lincoln's friends. Lincoln's shadow lay heavily over the Sangamon Valley of Masters's youth. But Masters's father was a liberal Democrat, religiously indifferent, and his own adversaries were frequently Republican and plutocratic. Even more important was Masters's admiration for Stephen A. Douglas, who had served as the real protagonist of the novel Children of the Market Place and whom Masters in an effusive essay proclaimed to be the only sane politician in the North.[19] Narveson argued that Masters had understandable reasons for writing a negative book on Lincoln, but even he could not explain the biographer's virulent tone.

Masters's third biographical venture was a rare opportunity for him, and the result was one of his best books. Vachel Lindsay, Springfield-born, was ten years younger but an Illinois poet and a personal if not an intimate friend. Although vastly different in temperament and in intellectual equipment, the two men shared the same background and the same devotion to the profession of a poet. As Masters said in the introduction to his biography, "I understood, perhaps, better than any one, the character of his environment, the quality of the people among whom he lived." Moreover, the book that he published in 1935 was something of a command performance. For Mrs. Lindsay, shortly after her husband's suicide, asked Masters to write Lindsay's life and offered to make available to him a mass of documentary material--letters, diaries, notebooks. She placed no restrictions on his use of this cache of papers and in no way influenced his interpretation. Masters certainly did not see eye to eye with Lindsay about many things; moreover, he was frank enough to say that Lindsay had no sense of logic and that he accepted an emotional religion which made him myopic to reality. But "Lindsay's ancestry, his education, his religion, his morals, his tastes were Middle West," peculiarly American and similar, despite some fundamental differences, to Masters's own.[20] The book which he wrote with his usual rapidity has certain faults. Some of the important evidence about Lindsay, notably about his childhood, was not immediately available. Lindsay had been an inveterate correspondent, especially in the years prior to his marriage, and these letters were not in his widow's possession. The biographer, furthermore, was inaccurate in such matters as dates and chronology. Even so, and despite the appearance of subsequent biographies with richer factual material, Masters's study remains the best book we have about one of the most fantastic figures in American poetry.

Reviewers were quick to see the importance of the work and to praise its author. No single book by Masters

received such consistent adulation. After all, the publication of a biography by a poet of Masters's stature about one
of the most publicized figures in American literature of the
twentieth century was a most uncommon event. Even more
to the point, the book was an important comment on the role
of the artist in American culture by one who was himself
deeply involved.

One of the earliest important reviews was by Hazelton Spencer, who himself had written an appreciative article
on Lindsay three years earlier.21 He pointed out that many
lives of Lindsay were possible: Lindsay as reformer, Lindsay as prophet, Lindsay as pure lyric poet. Masters had
produced a book which was sympathetic and understanding
but neither sentimental nor adulatory. Spencer thought that
anyone remotely interested in American culture would need
to read the book, a volume which he claimed would never be
totally superseded. And he added that it was a disgrace that
the greatest American poet since Whitman had never received his due from American critics.

Horace Gregory commented that Masters had mis-
dated The Art of the Motion Picture and was probably inaccurate in other details. Nevertheless he was enthusiastic
about the biography. He was rather amused by the idea of
a small town lawyer-atheist-iconoclast (Masters) writing a
tribute to the village preacher (Lindsay), although he insisted
that no one had better understanding than Masters of Lindsay's cultural background. Gregory drew a vivid picture of
the Springfield poet performing: "a sandy-haired man in a
blue serge suit, with the fire of an evangelist, must be
standing on the platform; he must not be tired, he must not
lose confidence, he must hear the people answer with ap-
plause." The tragedy was that this picture could hardly be
permanent; the time would come when the people would be
bored and Lindsay would tremble with fatigue and nervous
exhaustion. Gregory pointed out that Lindsay was not well
prepared to be a poet at all; consistently dominated by a religious, clubwoman mother, he was conventionally reared,
imperfectly educated, and often half-starved in his early maturity. Masters realized all this and wrote his biography
accordingly. But the result was superior. Gregory concluded, "This life of Lindsay should become a permanent addition to any library of American biography and collectors
should regard it as an invaluable item in Americana."22

Eda Lou Walton's review in the Nation was even more

laudatory. She termed the Masters study "one of the most interesting and fantastic biographies in contemporary American literature." She pointed out that the biographer, who tried to reform the Middle West after his own concept of freedom from middle-class morality and sectionalism, had written the life of a poet who consecrated himself to the building of a spiritual utopia in Springfield. Masters's outline of Lindsay's life, documented as it was by letters and diaries, she found fascinating. Masters could draw attention to Lindsay's illogical thinking without becoming unsympathetic. Miss Walton drew a parallel between Whitman and Lindsay with their mutual beliefs in equality, social justice, and Jeffersonian democracy, yet she argued that Lindsay had come on the scene too late. He was a Christian socialist who found his heroes destroyed, his religion unpracticed. The consequent frustration, as Masters clearly pointed out, helped to bring about Lindsay's suicide. 23

Two shorter reviews in religious periodicals emphasized Masters's hostility to Lindsay's simple faith but agreed that the biographer had been surprisingly fair in presenting the case. W. E. Garrison thought that two basic passions motivated Lindsay: a love of beauty with a desire to make it the common possession of man, and a deep antipathy toward social injustice. Masters, fully assisted by the poet's widow, showed clearly Lindsay's regrettable inconsistencies and weaknesses. Unable to understand Lindsay's simple piety, Masters probably attributed some of the poet's errors falsely to his Campbellite religion and needlessly ranted about Prohibition in his book. But he had produced nevertheless an honest study of the most American poet America has possessed. 24 Kenton Kilmer came to the same conclusion in his Commonweal review. The fact that Masters and Lindsay were friends, compatriots, and fellow poets made the first the ideal biographer of the second. The book contained valuable material, much of it furnished by Mrs. Lindsay; and the result was probably the definitive biography of the most American of our poets. 25

One of the most interesting assessments of the book came from Harriet Monroe. She had known both poets during their early productive years, had carried on extensive correspondence with each, and had welcomed the work of both to the pages of her journal Poetry. She began her review with the statement that the biography was "one of those profound searchings of the human soul which are rarely to be found in literature or any other art." Moreover, it was written about a man of genius by another man of genius who was "fully equipped by a powerful intelligence to understand both the exaltations and the limitations of the poet." Miss Monroe commented that she had learned that some of the Lindsay relatives were dissatisfied with the book because of certain inadequacies and omissions of important details, yet she emphasized Mrs. Lindsay's cooperation in supplying both diaries and correspondence.   Lindsay, of course, had flaws as a writer; "Lindsay's imagination got in the way of his intellect." As the poet himself once remarked, his thoughts were often sparse but his visions came in cataracts. Masters showed clearly the confusion of much of Lindsay's thinking as well as the forces of greed, vanity, and cultural prejudice against which he struggled so futilely. Miss Monroe found the biography perceptive, intuitively sympathetic, and frequently quotable.   Her real reservation was a purely personal one.   Masters had not taken the trouble to trace Lindsay's relationship with Poetry or to acknowledge that Lindsay had been awarded substantial monetary prizes by the magazine at a time when he was seriously in debt.   Masters had not even bothered to read the sheaf of letters which Lindsay had sent to Harriet Monroe over the years! 26

Another personal touch appeared in a notice which John Drinkwater contributed to the English Quarterly Review. Drinkwater had visited Lindsay at Springfield in 1919, at which time the poet had given him his personal copy of Spoon River Anthology inscribed with his own written comment: "no better poetry has ever come out of America, and no better book."   Drinkwater thought that Masters was well qualified to write the biography and clearly able to understand the spiritual gallantry and fearless patriotism that motivated Lindsay.   Although Drinkwater found the Springfield poet personally attractive he was certainly not unaware of his intellectual limitations, or as he put it, "the woolly and rhetorical elements in Lindsay's character that frustrated much of his purpose."   Masters's book was valuable despite its lack of clear continuity.   Drinkwater thought that Lindsay's life was such a compendium of threads and patches that a biographer would have trouble making it into an orderly narrative.   Real significance was found only in occasional words and in the vagrant moods of highest inspiration.   Drinkwater ended his review by stating his agreement with Masters that society had a duty to support its geniuses rather than to permit them to suffer from neglect and poverty. 27

A review by John Herbert Nelson in the academic

quarterly, _American Literature_, was more sober in tone than the reviews previously cited but was nevertheless laudatory. Nelson thought that Masters was the proper biographer of Lindsay and that he had adroitly used the material supplied him by Mrs. Lindsay. Nelson pointed out quite correctly that the account of Lindsay's boyhood was sketchy and unsatisfactory; on the other hand, Masters had done a superlative job in delineating Lindsay's emotional and intellectual experiences as a young man. Nelson also praised the biographer for his honest presentation of the facts about Lindsay's sexual inhibitions, his immaturity of mind, his marital difficulties, indeed all the circumstances which preceded his suicide. The reviewer felt that if Masters had not always been successful in excluding his personal prejudices, he had not allowed them to distort the main biographical story. Indeed, Nelson claimed that the book was praiseworthy and Masters's strongest prose volume.28

With three biographies behind him Masters chose his own life as the theme for his next prose venture. _Across Spoon River_, which he published in 1936, describes his youth and early maturity in considerable detail and carries the story down to 1917. Masters was often reluctant to give dates and identify people; thus the numerous women with whom he was involved have only first names, and Clarence Darrow, his Chicago law partner for many years, is never mentioned at all. On the other hand, he was specific in his attitude toward his family, toward Lewistown and Chicago, and he made no secret about the fact that although the law was his apparent profession, writing was the real occupation of his life. His long struggle to establish himself as a poet gives some cohesion to a narrative which is often disorderly and occasionally filled with a vague mysticism. Reviewers were puzzled by the book, yet conceded its importance as the revelation of a Middle Western life and as the chronicle of a poet in America.

The _Time_ review largely summarized the book's content and called it one of the grimmest records of literary success in American writing. Masters achieved the fame of _Spoon River Anthology_ only after emotional anguish, a liaison with a girl who subsequently killed herself, and divorce and the loss of his family. Readers would likely agree with the writer's contention that he was hypersensitive, yet their central impression was probably that a literary career was always a fearful struggle, at first disheartening and later hazardous.29 Eda Lou Walton thought that _Across Spoon_

River was a strange autobiography, virtually a case history. At once time Masters was famous, the most talked about literary figure in the Middle West, a national celebrity. But his hour of triumph was brief. The reviewer called attention to his early antagonism toward his background. His mother detested the small Middle Western towns, his father made rather a poor living, both parents seemed to favor his sister over him. Later, Masters himself hated his profession and the city to which he had gone for success. He sought solace among women, each of whom, as he put it, had her particular "aura," but his search did not produce happiness. Miss Walton claimed that he was badly educated and that he never became a good craftsman in verse. His success was due more to timeliness than to the merits of his poetry. In similar fashion the autobiography was so eccentric a book that its interest for readers was neither its style nor its subject but its revelation of a strange mind.[30] Floyd Dell was equally reluctant to praise it although he claimed that it gave interesting pictures of Chicago literati. Although Masters was refreshingly candid about sexual matters, Dell found his accounts of his amorous adventures drably monotonous. Indeed, he felt that the book did not do its subject justice. Once Masters was touched by Divine Fire; he could not explain the phenomenon; he only knew that it came and went.[31]

Much the same point of view was expressed by Carl Van Doren and Bernard De Voto. Van Doren remarked that once, for a few months, Masters ran side by side with Apollo.[32] In Chicago he was torn between two occupations, resorted to odd jobs to earn a living, was slow in discovering his true poetic idiom, and held unpopular opinions which handicapped his success as a lawyer. Van Doren noted that the autobiography went down only to Masters's forty-eighth year and that even then Masters had not reconciled some of his old intellectual conflicts. As a narrative it lacked steadiness but showed signs of the old turbulence and vitality. Van Doren pronounced the book honest and graceless rather than serene, "the blunt, ardent story of a troubled man finding out that he was a poet." Bernard De Voto came to much the same conclusion about what he termed this Delphic Apollo writing in an Illinois river bottom.[33] He called Across Spoon River the work of a man who had produced one of the decisive books of the time. In his biography of Lindsay Masters had discussed the native myths and symbols of the prairies, and to these his own experiences were also true. De Voto observed that Masters enumerated very typical situations which had strong symbolic value: the village boy transfixed by the ideal of writing poetry and being ridiculed as a sissy for liking books, work on a small town newspaper, village literary societies, a high school teacher who hoped to gain vicarious fame through the literary exploits of a star pupil, the impecunious lawyer devoting all his free hours to writing. In his review, however, De Voto virtually ignored the Chicago years, Masters's romantic adventures, and indeed the incoherent structure of the book.

Robert E. Spiller's review in American Literature not only evaluated the book but tried to place it and its author within a cultural framework. Across Spoon River, he said, belonged with Dreiser's A Book About Myself and Anderson's A Story Teller's Story as a record of a literary era now closed, an invaluable document of a period when writers experienced a special kind of frustration and when the prevalent naturalism was coarse but somewhat superficial. He pointed out that Masters had never been noted for restraint and that the story told in his autobiography was characteristic. If Masters's life had been a succession of disappointments and blind lunges, it was certainly not the result of inhibitions. The father had been a rebel against the farm and manual labor; the son rebelled equally against the village and the law. Masters, writing in his sixties, could conclude rather proudly that his head was always bowed in the attitude of attack. Spiller called Across Spoon River "a sincere and frank exposition of a baffled soul." Masters did give personal and vivid pictures of the coterie of poets associated with Harriet Monroe's magazine, of Dreiser and Sandburg and Lindsay. He told a significant story and he told it honestly, but not always with clarity and understanding.34

The two final biographies which Masters published in 1937 and 1938 dealt with authors who had deeply influenced him and whom to some extent he imitated. Whitman had been one of his chief models in the writing of poetry; Mark Twain had provided him with a framework and perhaps even episodes and characters for his early fiction. Of the two men he felt closest to Whitman, many of whose ideas he accepted. Twain he admired but often disagreed with. Both books were widely noticed but the reviews lacked any clear consensus; the gamut of criticism varied from the frankly disapproving to the laudatory.

Allen Tate, in a brief review in _Poetry_, commented that Masters was unequipped as a literary critic to write a biography of Whitman and claimed that as a consequence he had produced a curiously muddled book. Although he was not specific in his charges, since he admitted that he was not a Whitman specialist, Tate could speak only with scorn of the Masters study. He noted that Masters had presented somewhat incoherently Whitman's limitations, among which was agnosticism, and then added that he found it curious that so good a book as _Spoon River Anthology_ should have been written by the village atheist.[35] Newton Arvin, who the next year published his own study of Whitman, claimed that Masters had obviously chosen an uncongenial subject. Why, he asked, did the biographer crowd so much familiar material into his book--extracts from Traubel's diary, long quotations from Whitman's prose works, all easily acces- sible? Masters was guilty of factual errors, inconsisten- cies, and highly debatable if not patently false statements. Moreover, his psychological interpretations were not new. Arvin declared that Masters might be forgiven for such faults if he had added substantially to our understanding of Whitman; in his opinion this had not been done.[36] Andrew Corry, in _Commonweal_, conceded that at least for the mom- ent Masters had presented the significant facts of Whitman's life. He had written charmingly about the Long Island boy- hood and family background and sensitively about the Civil War hospital experiences. Nor did Masters conceal Whit- man's faults: childish boasting, coarseness, occasional un- organized inarticulateness. In general, Corry rather ap- proved of the picture Masters drew of Whitman as person- ality and poet.[37]

Other reviewers were more enthusiastic. Peter Monro Jack's comments were somewhat evasive but on the whole approving. He observed that Masters's books on Lindsay and Whitman had certain similarities and might well have been bound together: both in a sense were pleas for Americanism in poetry and criticism. The Whitman volume was disappointing as a study of the verse, since Masters was obviously more interested in the relationship of Whit- man to American history. He thought that Whitman's vision of America, despite contradictions and ambiguities, was al- so Masters's vision. But he found a curious illogicality in the biographer's thinking. Masters seemed to argue that Whitman would be a great poet only if America had followed his pronouncements. Since the common man obviously did not respond to Whitman's verse there was some question about the poet's real stature. In any event, the poetry remained and the bard had disciples, among them Sandburg, Hart Crane, and Masters himself.38 Clifton Joseph Furness thought that Masters's biography was an enjoyable reading experience, an honest, even reverent book grounded in research but unfortunately not documented. Like other reviewers, Furness objected to the excessive quotation. Yet he observed that Masters had given a clear picture of Whitman and sex and had considered adequately the influences on the poet of Quakerism, mysticism, and religion. In sharp contrast to Allen Tate's captious remarks, Furness approved of the literary criticism as a real contribution to the book. He concluded that after the aberration of his book on Lincoln, the Masters of Spoon River Anthology had returned.39

Eda Lou Walton also disagreed with some of the negative comments. To her Masters was less interested in Whitman's political theories than in the poetry. The books on Lindsay and Whitman provided an instructive contrast. Lindsay needed defense as well as elucidation. Whitman required no such apology and Masters could be more objective and less personal in a study which was the most comprehensive life of Whitman that had so far appeared. Like Furness, the reviewer observed that Masters did not hesitate to point out faults, and he had made a case for Whitman as being sexually subnormal. The biography, to be sure, had faults; Miss Walton called it repetitive, rambling, and over-crammed with quotations. Nevertheless, it was the most human and complete study of Whitman available; the biographer had done a superlative job in describing the poet's final years, his illness and his death.40

With this judgment Mark Van Doren was in complete accord.41 The book was written freely and somewhat carelessly, but even though it contained a ton of documents it was still "the best general account of the poet to date." Masters, according to Van Doren, neither gushed nor condescended. Although he admired Whitman, he realized that the poet had written very few first-rate poems and that he was certainly not free from such faults as vanity and childishness. Van Doren remarked that the volume did not rest on its literary criticism but was a notable general account.

Two brief reviews from across the Atlantic Ocean might also be cited here. Seán O'Faoláin in the Spectator said little about the plan, comprehensiveness, and reliability of the biography but was inclined to interpret it as an example of what he called nationalistic criticism. Masters's view of Whitman as an apostle of Jeffersonianism gave the study a certain freshness and vigor. Moreover, at bottom he had provided a rounded picture of the Good Gray Poet.42 The London Times Literary Supplement remarked that neither a sensationalist nor a psychoanalyst would get much satisfaction out of Masters's biography. There were, furthermore, no new revelations. But in discussing Whitman's sexual life and his Civil War experiences Masters had shown both an impartial fairness and a sense of proportion. The biographer also displayed insight and comprehension in his interpretation of Whitman. The book was certainly not without faults: Masters seemed jejune in his comments on Whitman's cosmic religion and made extravagant claims for Whitman's judgments of men and literature. Fortunately, though, Masters did not dwell unduly on Whitman's narcissism. The review concluded with the remark that "a biographer who appreciates his subject's greatness may be forgiven much."43

Certainly such a judgment could have been made by no one who read Masters's life of Lincoln, and probably not by anyone familiar with the life of Mark Twain. Indeed, Masters's Mark Twain, a Portrait, published in 1938, is almost as puzzling a book as his study of the martyred president. In many ways biographer and biographee resembled each other: both were born in the Middle West, spent their early lives in small towns with a provincial culture, had a limited formal education which they endeavored to supplement by wide reading, took a somewhat sceptical view of the American scene, and after a great popular success produced a stream of books many of which were assailed for carelessness and incoherence. Moreover, each man trained for a profession which he early relinquished (Twain, of course, enjoyed being a steamboat pilot, whereas Masters hated the law), and both became to some extent the victims of their prejudices. Masters admired some of Mark Twain's work enough to imitate it; certainly Mitch Miller and its sequels would never have existed if they had not been preceded by Tom Sawyer and Huckleberry Finn. Nevertheless, when Masters came to write his biographical portrait of Twain he castigated him unmercifully in language which H. L. Mencken would have delighted in calling a schimpflexikon. The result was that reviewers were almost unanimous in condemning the book.

Even the amount of space allowed reviewers of the

book is a reflection of the importance which editors gave it. Most of the reviews were brief, in some cases little more than notices, but they made Masters's bias and ill temper perfectly clear. Time called the book a polemical biography that went far beyond the reinterpretation of Twain provided earlier by Van Wyck Brooks. Indeed, Masters presented Twain as a clown whose genius was warped by his refusal to challenge the ruling powers.[44] The New Republic asserted that Masters had presented Twain as a misdirected genius who acquiesced in and flattered rather than satirizing the Gilded Age. Masters had done nothing which Van Wyck Brooks had not done more thoroughly and with greater sympathy and grace.[45] Milton Rugoff, in the Nation, claimed that Masters wrote with a bludgeon when he argued that Twain, with the ability to become a great satirist, ended up as a clown. Twain, in the biographer's view, waged war on petty frauds and deceptions but never rose to the heights to assail cruelty and superstition. Rugoff nevertheless took the position that Masters, fanatical as he was and writing with virtually no documentation, was yet justified in producing a challenging book which ought to appeal to the reader's social conscience.[46] M. L. Elting, in the Forum, was somewhat milder in his disapproval. Masters, he thought, had produced a portrait, not a biography, which gave a highly individualized interpretation of the boy from Missouri and which slurred Twain's achievements in order to stress his faults.[47]

But these reviews were rather superficial. It remained for others, especially the Mark Twain specialists, to write scathing denunciations. Eda Lou Walton called the book Masters's psychoanalysis of Twain, which she found readable but infuriating. Masters charged Twain with being de-southernized, de-westernized, and under the control of his wife, accusations of course which Van Wyck Brooks had made previously. Miss Walton conceded that Masters could be interesting if he had new material or new documents, but in this case he had neither. Instead, he was giving the reader a picture of his own prejudices, and he came perilously close to producing a caricature.[48]

Fred W. Lorch, an academic critic writing in American Literature, gave the book a careful scrutiny and came away with an even more negative verdict.[49] He enumerated Masters's charges against Twain and pointed out that the biographer's chief complaint against his subject was his failure to be something he had never tried to be: namely, a satirist exposing American economic, social, and political evils. Moreover, Masters had not familiarized himself with the extensive research done on Twain, nor had he bothered to be accurate in reporting facts or in quoting Twain's own words. Lorch concluded that since Masters's book had three serious faults, factual errors, unwarranted assumptions, and a confused philosophy, it did not deserve serious scholarly attention.

Edward Wagenknecht, who had himself written a book on Mark Twain in 1935, allowed Masters certain merits. He observed that the biographer knew the Middle West and gave a good account of early influences on Twain, that he had made some perceptive comments on the famous novels, and that he was surprisingly appreciative of the book on Joan of Arc and wildly enthusiastic about The Mysterious Stranger. Masters also was quite correct in denying Twain any coherent, consistent philosophy of life. The trouble was that most of this had been said before and that Masters was never able to support his accusations that Twain was a coward and a money-grabber. More serious were Masters's savage opposition to Christianity, his ignorance of most Twain scholarship, and his attribution of motives to the humorist which were purely conjecture. 'The famous indictment of Twain by Van Wyck Brooks was now old and utterly untenable; moreover, what Brooks could not do with a scalpel, Masters could hardly accomplish with a bludgeon. Wagenknecht remarked at the end of his review that Masters was so determined to stress what Twain was not that he completely forgot to consider what Twain was.50

Without question, however, the most devastating attack on the book was the work of Bernard De Voto, who had already written his own reply to Van Wyck Brooks.51 De Voto could hardly restrain his anger and contempt. He not only repeated the faults enumerated by Lorch and Wagenknecht in previous reviews, but he asserted that Masters was so insensitive to literary values that he was quite unqualified to write a book about Mark Twain. Factually erroneous and based on an utterly false interpretation of the great humorist, Masters's biography was "the most inaccurate, the most wildly incomprehensible, and the stupidest" yet published. Mark Twain was certainly not without faults, but Masters was incompetent to discuss them.

In contrast to these venomous American attacks the review in the London Times Literary Supplement was moderation itself. Twain's reputation, like that of Dickens, had reached the point where some correction might be in order. Masters indeed had made some astonishing allegations against Twain, among them buffoonery, commercialism, and a dishonest public conservatism which belied his inner convictions. But the reviewer implied that there was some basis for these remarks. He made no comment about the book's lack of documentation nor about its inaccuracy; indeed, he expressed no judgment about the general reliability of the work. 52

In several of his biographies as well as in some of the longer narrative poems Masters incorporated a good deal of history. This is not surprising when one realizes the extent of his reading in this field and the fact that he considered himself something of a specialist on the development of the United States before the Civil War. More than one critic in evaluating his work remarked that it was often overburdened with historical fact and political speculation, material which despite its intrinsic interest produced serious disproportion. But Masters never ventured to write a comprehensive history of a period or a campaign or a war. The closest he came was a rambling account of a city and a nostalgic reminiscence of a river.

The Tale of Chicago (1933) was the direct result of his thirty-years residence in the Windy City, a tale told primarily in personal terms. Masters had celebrated Chicago, its founders and its sights, in various short poems. In 1928 he had contributed an article, "Chicago: Yesterday, To-day and To-Morrow," to the Century Magazine. In various autobiographical statements and interviews he had expressed his attitude to the city where he had practiced law for many years and written some of his most successful poetry. This attitude was ambivalent. He told David Karsner that Chicago was his particular hell and therefore his stimulant to work. "I dislike it so actively that it acts as an irritant. To escape Chicago I seek refuge in my work there." 53 But to other persons he confessed that Chicago was a magical place of vitality and fascination. By 1933, after a dozen years away from the city, he felt compelled to write its story.

The result was not impressive. As usual Masters neglected sources, depended more upon memory than research, recorded more impressions than facts. He touched on many subjects, with general inadequacy. The book had a certain immediacy, since Masters could describe the city as he knew it in the 1890's and the early 1900's. But his failure even to mention Poetry: A Magazine of Verse in his sketchy survey of the cultural life of the city is representative of his biased approach. Lois Hartley called the book a readable volume, despite the fact that it was factually undependable and badly proportioned. After all, Masters had known the city for three decades.54 But reviewers in the major journals generally ignored the volume.

The Sangamon, Masters's mellowest prose volume and his last book to appear during his lifetime, was published in 1942. The sixteenth volume in the well known Rivers of America series, it dealt with a river which had only vicarious fame. The Sangamon was never navigable; it had not been the site of battles or industry; it was not even particularly scenic, but rather a shallow, meandering prairie stream which reached the Illinois River south of Havana. But the Sangamon Valley was Masters's home during his youth, and for some decades before that the shadow of Lincoln had brought it greatness.

A brief New Yorker notice called the Sangamon River the genius loci of Masters's New Salem country and termed Masters's writing genuinely evocative, with a deep filial devotion to the prairie neighborhood.55 R. L. Duffus wrote a gentle and friendly review for the New York Times in which he remarked that Masters's Sangamon country never really existed but on the other hand would never die from the American memory. Masters had more to say about Menard County than about the river and more comments about the people (notably the associates of Lincoln) than about the county. But even though Masters strove to define the valley as the center of Jeffersonian idealism in the west, he wrote most effectively about its physical loveliness, somewhat amiably distorted by memory.56 Lloyd Lewis, a special student of Lincoln, remarked that Masters had treated Illinois' greatest figure somewhat evasively but commended him for his lyrically nostalgic picture of a region which he had loved in his boyhood. Lewis also thought that Masters had provided tone poems about such figures as John Armstrong, Jack Kelso, and Anne Rutledge.57 In a somewhat more objective evaluation Lois Hartley mentioned the rambling narrative often interrupted by autobiographical bits, the occasional irrelevant passages, and the almost total lack of organization. But she, too, felt that the Sangamon book had vividness and charm.58

Biography

It is certainly appropriate here to quote Masters's own words about his last prose volume: "Naturally the country possessed my imagination ... It may be that I idealize it, but at any rate it has a magical appeal to me quite beyond my power to describe. I loved the people there then and I love their memory."59

Notes

1. ELM, "Histories of the American Mind," American Mercury (July, 1935), 35: 341.

2. Lois Hartley, "Edgar Lee Masters--Biographer and Historian," Journal of the Illinois State Historical Society (Spring, 1961), 54: 56-83.

3. Hartley, op. cit., 67.

4. Hartley, op. cit., 58.

5. Time (February 16, 1931), 17: 15, No. 7.

6. American Mercury (April, 1931), 22: vi.

7. Outlook (February 18, 1931), 157: 267.

8. Review of Reviews (March, 1931), 83: 16.

9. William MacDonald, "Find Lincoln," Nation (March 4, 1931), 132: 246-247.

10. H. L. Mencken, "The Birth of Order," New York Herald Tribune Books (February 8, 1931), 1-2.

11. Catholic World (April, 1931), 133: 115.

12. Edgar Dewitt Jones, "Not A Masterpiece," Christian Century (April 1, 1931), 48: 450.

13. Don C. Seitz, Bookman (April, 1931), 73: 198-200.

14. W. M. Quaife, Mississippi Valley Historical Review (September, 1931), 18: 260-262.

15. Claude Bowers, Saturday Review of Literature (February 21, 1931), 7: 609-610.

16. London Times Literary Supplement (October 15, 1931), 786.

17. Charles Willis Thompson, "A Belittling Life of Lincoln by Edgar Lee Masters," New York Times Book Review (February 8, 1931), 193: 5.

18. Robert D. Narveson, "The Two Lincolns of Edgar Lee Masters," Discourse (Winter, 1961), 4: 20-39. See also John T. Flanagan, "Three Illinois Poets," Centennial Review (Fall, 1972), 16: 313-327.

19. ELM, "Stephen A. Douglas," American Mercury (January, 1931), 22: 11-23.

20. ELM, Vachel Lindsay, A Poet in America (New York and London, 1935), Introduction, vii.

21. Hazelton Spencer, "An Amazing Tragedy," Saturday Review of Literature (September 8, 1935), 12: 7, No. 22. Cf. Spencer, "The Life and Death of Vachel Lindsay," American Mercury (April, 1932), 25: 455-462.

22. Horace Gregory, "A Poet Indigenous to the American Soil," New York Herald Tribune Books (October 6, 1935), 5.

23. Eda Lou Walton, "Utopia in Springfield," Nation (October 23, 1935), 141: 477.

24. W. E. Garrison, "The Most American Poet," Christian Century (October 30, 1935), 52: 1377-1378.

25. Kenton Kilmer, "Butterfly Souls and the Y.M.C.A.," Commonweal (December 13, 1935), 23: 194-195.

26. H[arriet] M[onroe], "The Lindsay Biography," Poetry: A Magazine of Verse (March, 1936), 47: 337-344.

27. John Drinkwater, "Two American Lives," Quarterly Review (January, 1936), 266: 132-135.

28. John Herbert Nelson, American Literature (November, 1936), 8: 340.

29. Time (November 16, 1936), 28: 116-117, No. 20.

30. Eda Lou Walton, "The Man from Spoon River Tells His Own Story," New York Times Book Review (November 8, 1936), 4.

31. Floyd Dell, "Spoon River's Barren Soil," New York Herald Tribune Books (November 8, 1936), 4.

32. Carl Van Doren, "Behind Spoon River," Nation (November 14, 1936), 143:580.

33. Bernard De Voto, "Delphic Apollo in Illinois," Saturday Review of Literature (November 14, 1936), 15: 5, No. 3.

34. Robert E. Spiller, American Literature (March, 1937), 9: 102-3.

35. Allen Tate, "Whitman in America," Poetry: A Magazine of Verse (September, 1937), 50: 350-353.

36. Newton Arvin, "Whitman As He Was Not," New Republic (April 14, 1937), 90: 301-312.

37. Andrew Corry, "Uranian Indecision," Commonweal (May 7, 1937), 26: 52-53.

38. Peter Monro Jack, "Walt Whitman's Fresh Vision of a Pioneer America," New York Times Book Review (March 7, 1937), 5.

39. Clifton Joseph Furness, "Spokesman of America," Saturday Review of Literature (March 27, 1937), 15: 7, No. 22.

40. Eda Lou Walton, "Whitman Reconsidered," Nation (March 20, 1937), 144: 330-331.

41. Mark Van Doren, "Plowing Through Whitman," New York Herald Tribune Books (February 28, 1937), 7.

42. Seán O'Faoláin, "The Good Gray Poet," Spectator (April 23, 1937), 158: 769-770.

43. London Times Literary Supplement (June 12, 1937), No. 1, 845, 442.

44. Time (February 28, 1938), 31: 71, No. 9.

45. New Republic (March 2, 1938), 94: 112.

46. Milton Rugoff, "Safe Water," Nation (August 6, 1938), 147: 134.

47. M. L. Elting, Forum (April, 1938), 99: vii, No. 4.

48. Eda Lou Walton, "Biography in the Mirror," New York Herald Tribune Books (February 27, 1938), 10.

49. Fred W. Lorch, American Literature (November, 1938), 10: 373-376.

50. Edward Wagenknecht, "Mr. Masters on Mark Twain," New York Times Book Review (May 8, 1938), 10.

51. Bernard De Voto, "Mark Twain: A Caricature," Saturday Review of Literature (March 19, 1938), 17: 5, No. 21.

52. "Mark Twain and His Market," London Times Literary Supplement (April 2, 1938), No. 1, 887.

53. David Karsner, Sixteen Authors to One (New York, 1928), 132.

54. Lois Hartley, op. cit., 80.

55. New Yorker (June 6, 1942), 18: 64, No. 16.

56. R. L. Duffus, "The Scenes and the People Abe Lincoln Knew," New York Times Book Review (June 14, 1942), 3.

57. Lloyd Lewis, "Sleepy Prairie River Shrine," New York Herald Tribune Books (June 21, 1942), 4.

58. Lois Hartley, op. cit., 83.

59. ELM, The Sangamon (New York, 1942), 116.

CHAPTER 9

LATER VERSE

Masters was always a prodigious worker, unquestionably too prolific for his own good but the creator of a flood of miscellaneous verse ever since his adolescent period when he contributed poems to various Illinois newspapers. Not all of this verse has been collected into volumes, but the best of these occasional pieces were reprinted in book form between 1930 and 1942. Acknowledgements in the several florilegia suggest the wide distribution of his magazine verse; the periodicals to which he contributed included the *American Mercury*, *Scribner's*, the *Century*, *Poetry*: *A Magazine of Verse*, *Asia*, *Today*, *Commonweal*, and the *Independent*. It might be observed that the *American Mercury* published not only about a dozen of the Chinatown squibs later collected in *Lichee Nuts* but also the generally admired longer poem entitled "Beethoven's Ninth Symphony and the King Cobra." Masters's two final books of poetry, each less than a hundred pages in length, came from the press of James A. Decker at Prairie City, Illinois, a location which, as the poet himself pointed out, was only a few miles away from such places as Bernadotte, Lewistown, and Havana, all of which were named in the poems.

Lichee Nuts, published by Horace Liveright in 1930, is a kind of tour de force in the Masters canon, a slim collection of about a hundred anecdotes, sketches, shrewd or satiric observations phrased in pidgin English and capitalizing on the false orientalism which was much in vogue at the time. The caption "Confucius say" was a convenient tag for the purpose of introducing jests, wisecracks, tart generalizations, or superficial profundities. Masters seldom used the tag itself but followed the convention in introducing such characters as Tuck High, Wing Lee, Li Chien, Hi Ho, Hip Tung, and Sun Wet, whose activities he described briefly and to whom he attributed occasionally salty observations. There is more than a touch of Spoon River in these vignettes. Certainly it is not hard to hear the tone of the famous cemetery in the speech of some of Masters's almond-eyed characters. Thus Yang Chung philosophizes, "Denial has as much sensation as indulgence"; Yet Wei remarks, "What you give, must be measured by what you don't give"; and Wah Tom comments in language which must reflect the thought of his creator:

> ...women are the same as pictures,
> If you love pictures you want more than one;
> If you love women you want more than one.[1]

The reader will note with amusement that this salient observation is made to Elmer Chubb, Masters's alter ego who occasionally deigned to visit Chinatown.

Lichee Nuts did not attract wide attention and has since been completely forgotten. But the few reviewers who noticed the book were quietly amused and recognized to their surprise a side of Masters which was not generally apparent. Lichee Nuts also confirmed Masters's ability to use the formula multum in parvo, to return in other words to the memorable brevity and concision of Spoon River Anthology despite a radical change of locale.

William Rose Benét, not always an admirer of Masters, found many pleasing touches in Lichee Nuts. He devoted much of his weekly column, "Round About Parnassus," to comment about the denizens of Chinatown whom Masters drew and observed that the poet had succeeded very well in conveying the Chinese attitude of passivity steeped in a deep philosophy. Indeed Benét liked the characterizations so much that he finished the book with regret; he expressed his disappointment at having to leave so soon these "mellow though trenchant friends."[2]

An anonymous reviewer in the New York Times remarked that Masters had capitalized on the current fondness for Chinese poetry and lichee nuts in a way that could hardly fail to please readers. If Masters's wisdom was not quite equal to that of Confucius, the poet had at least succeeded in drawing such characters from the Mott Street environment as Hip Lung and Yuan Chang and Sun Wet with humorous impact. The reviewer especially liked the obituary of the art impresario, Hip Lung. Realizing that his death was imminent, Hip Lung chose one of his art treasures and sat in the window "with the vase of nephrite/ Folded about with his cold dead hands."[3]

Ruth Lechlitner pointed out in her review that Masters had visited New York's Chinatown and had returned with samples of celestial wit and wisdom. Moreover, he had isolated the inhabitants of Chinatown from their traditional laundries, tea shops, and joss houses in order to use them as mediums for satire and irony. Thus the Chinese served as the vehicle for Masters to ridicule Christian evangelism, materialism, and chauvinism. Miss Lechlitner particularly liked the tart parody of Whitman: "To have great audiences/ There must be fewer poets."[4]

During the years when Masters was otherwise busy with biography, fiction, and narrative verse, he yet managed to publish five book of miscellaneous poetry, at least one of which, Invisible Landscapes (1935), received remarkably favorable reviews. The book resembled some of the collections he had published twenty years earlier in its combination of classical themes, celebrations of places, abstractions, and nostalgic scenes, and the metrical forms were equally varied. Many of the passages show the poet's usual haste and carelessness. "The Seven Cities of America" (Boston, New York, Charleston, New Orleans, San Francisco, Salt Lake City, Chicago) is a paean to American urban shrines written as a free verse catalogue, while "Give Us Back Our Country" calls for a return to the older republic when corruption, greed, and crime were not dominant; and "Beethoven's Ninth Symphony and the King Cobra" deals with the problem of evil. Sandwiched in with these longer poems are sincere reminiscences of the Illinois prairie country, such as "Concord Church" and "Sandridge" and "The Old Farm," in which the reader finds no notes of asperity. In these recreations of an environment the Mason County Hills become almost a leit-motif.

W. E. Garrison remarked in the Christian Century that Masters had extended the scope of his thought since the appearance of the anthology; he was no longer a cynic and he seemed more concerned with man than with men. In no other way, the reviewer thought, could the attention to evolution, psychology, and behaviorism be accounted for.[5] Wilbert Snow made somewhat the same comment since he found Invisible Landscapes full of reflective and expository poetry in which Masters had apparently abandoned dramatic character portrayal for speculations about existence itself.6 Snow conceded that occasionally the poet seemed to prefer essays to verse, and he claimed that Masters resembled a fierce individualist who was trying to make peace with his tribe. But the volume contained excellent verse, notably in "Indian Corn Dance" and "Beethoven's Ninth Symphony and the King Cobra." William Rose Benét praised the same poems in his review and pointed out that Masters showed power even in his most controversial verse, for example, "I Smell the Blood of a Christian Man." Benét thought that Masters was at his best in free verse; when he chose to write in rhyme he frequently got off key and became guilty of cacophony and triteness of which he seemed unaware. The critic expressed considerable doubt about Masters's artistic taste but contended that no one could question his sincerity or earnestness in regard to truth.7

A notice in the Christian Science Monitor observed that the book reflected Masters's sense of landscape with past associations. Instead of being dramatic or even lyrical, Invisible Landscapes showed narrative, descriptive, and meditative qualities reminiscent of Wordsworth. Such poems as "Hymn to Nature" and "Hymn to Earth" particularly suggested the Lake Poet. The critic agreed with other reviewers that "Beethoven's Ninth Symphony and the King Cobra" was the most remarkable poem in the volume and argued that on the whole the collection revealed some of Masters's early rebelliousness but that it was now "tinged with melancholy rather than anger and with sentiment rather than tragedy."8

To Peter Monro Jack, on the other hand, the title poem of Invisible Landscapes was as fine a poem as anything that Masters had written, one of the first modern poems, indeed, to reveal the enduring strength of the landscape. The poet had successfully combined a mystical love of nature with the pleasure experienced in actual places. Here there was no touch of the acerbity of Spoon River; instead, Masters remembered with a deep joy the Sangamon Valley locations of his youth.9

Two brief notices in English periodicals also drew attention to Invisible Landscapes. Dilys Powell in the Spectator remarked that "Evolution and a bit of pantheism help out Mr. Edgar Lee Masters's America-conscious Invisible Landscapes."10 The London Times Literary Supplement ob-

jected to Masters's tendency in these poems to write philosophical discourses or even to indulge in scientific lectur-
ing. The anonymous reviewer observed that the poet's
themes were often loosely elaborated and that imagination
unfortunately got entangled in abstract reasoning. But he
admitted that poems like "Concord Church" and "The Old
Farm" were sincere and effective interpretations of abodes
close to the writer's heart, while "Beethoven's Ninth Symphony and the King Cobra" dealt with the theme of evil with
astonishing power.11

The most enthusiastic review was Philip Blair Rice's in
the Nation.12 Rice perceived in Invisible Landscapes a certain weariness and even undertones of resignation or defeat,
which he found inevitable in a sensitive and courageous man
who had long espoused individualism and liberalism. Nevertheless, the book, judged not as a doctrinaire performance
but simply as poetry, was possibly Masters's finest work.
Rice praised the rhymed poems for their fluency, the blank
verse for its suppleness, and the free cadences for their intimate relationship with the thought expressed. "The best
pieces in it have a lyrical quality which he has achieved
hitherto in only a few scattered lines, and even those passages which are not designed to sing manifest a grace and
sureness of diction whose absence has marred much of his
previous work." Rice concluded that Masters's lyrical genius had apparently flowered late; he called Invisible Landscapes a memorable volume.

In 1936 and 1939 Masters published two volumes,
Poems of People and More People, which might well be considered a single work and which elicited similar comments
from most reviewers. Leisurely portraits of men, lacking
both the concision and the bitterness of the Spoon River epitaphs, provide the substance of these books, and the poems
have a certain mellowness which was certainly not distin-
guishable in the earlier Masters. The subjects reveal an
astonishing scope. There are poems about such remote
sages as Catullus and Confucius. Black Hawk, Aaron Burr,
and George Rogers Clark evoked tributes, while the roll of
American heroes includes Washington, Jefferson, Daniel
Boone, Emerson, Andrew Jackson, the explorer Meriwether
Lewis, the naval commander Lawrence, and the clipper ship
builder Donald McKay. But the bulk of the verse is given
over to portraits of the simpler persons, the retired steel
workers and farmers and lawyers and politicians who live
out their lives in nostalgic recollections, drinking in taverns

or watching at a distance the events in which they can no longer be active. Masters was sympathetic and perceptive in his characterization of such figures as Jake Mann, Peter Van Zuylen, Lute Crockett, and Old Georgie Kirby. All of them resembled, to use Oliver Wendell Holmes's analogy, last leaves on the tree. Masters drew them, sometimes awkwardly to be sure, but with skill. As usual his metrical forms in the two collections include blank verse, rhymed quatrains, and an irregular free verse which is sometimes merely rearranged prose.

Time noticed Poems of People and Carl Sandburg's The People, Yes in the same review and devoted only a few lines to Masters's book. Masters himself was described "as a gruff, hard-bitten, Kansas-born lawyer whose poems were bitter epitaphs on the wasted lives of a small town." Most of the poems, the reviewer thought, were full of stock attitudes; only in the tribute to Andrew Jackson did the poet make his title come alive.13 William Rose Benét gave grudging praise to the new book. He admitted that Masters was at home in many fields of American history and that he had read enormously, but contended that the poetry was less important than the substance. On the other hand, Masters's genuine narrative ability sometimes appeared in these poems, especially in "Iolanthe" and "Zelley's Bar."12 Ben Belitt, writing in the Nation, was somewhat more caustic. The patriotic eulogies were full of limping lines relieved occasionally by interesting aphorisms, and the book as a whole showed triviality. Belitt obviously preferred the Spoon River types who were occasionally memorialized here, since Masters expressed in these portraits his contempt for much of the shallowness and greed of modern life and insisted on such stoic virtues as self-reliance.15

Two English reviews of Poems of People were moderately enthusiastic. The notice in the London Times Literary Supplement pointed out that the book included two types of poems: celebrations of standard American heroes like Jefferson and Jackson, and vignettes of simple folk, most of whom were decent people but who suffered from thwarted ideals and crushed hopes. The reviewer could not ignore what he considered Masters's crude and casual style, but he found a strong human appeal in the poetry.16 Michael Roberts, in the Spectator, praised Masters for his ability in narrative and characterization, qualities which were lacking in contemporary British verse. He also felt that whether the portraits were of conventional heroes or of ordinary folk they had a certain vividness. Again, however, Roberts objected to Masters's disdain of verbal skill. As he put it, Masters was popular "because it is not necessary to have any feeling for the poetic qualities of words in order to appreciate his poems."17

A rather long review by Kerker Quinn drew attention to the wide range of characters in Poems of People as well as the variety of characterization. Masters showed technical mastery in utilizing "monologue, dramatic dialogue, group-tin-type, memoir, epitaph, contrast of the present person with his past self, portrait of the person's mind, ideals, environs, everyday behavior or conspicuous deeds." Quinn also observed that the poet seemed less interested in characterization for its own sake than in the opportunity it gave him to express a moralistic judgment. He clearly admired the individualists, the fighters for freedom; and he obviously preferred the unsophisticated era before the arrival of monopoly and big industry.18

Reviews of More People, which followed the original collection by three years, were brief and casual. Desmond Hawkins simply reported in the Spectator that Masters had collected a further volume of character sketches and "potted biographies."19 The notice in the London Times Literary Supplement was entitled "Simple Folk" and complained about the shallowness of the poetry, filled as it was with commonplace and insignificant statements. The reviewer observed perceptively that Masters had always depended more on revealing statements than on suggestive images. But only in such poems as "Elkins' Shack" and "Peter Van Zuylen" did the method really seem to work.20

Harry Roskolenko's review in Poetry contrasted Masters's verse about the Middle West with Frost's and Robinson's poetry about New England. To him the ghost of Spoon River was still apparent in the poems of More People. But though he quoted at length from such pieces as "Jake Mann" he said little of consequence about the book.21

Masters's final two books of verse, both the products of a private press, won only scattered recognition, although some of the reviewers appreciated the warm nostalgia of various tributes to the Illinois landscape. Illinois Poems, published in 1941, elicited a few brief notices. Along the Illinois, which appeared the next year, was completely disregarded by the major reviewing media.

Coleman Rosenberger combined notices of Illinois Poems and John G. Neihardt's Song of Jed Smith in his Poetry review. The Masters volume he termed the postscript to a long career. Rosenberger commented chiefly on the themes of the poems; the political verse was disquieting and obviously partisan, whereas some of the celebrations of places and events had undeniable charm. He especially approved of "Concord Church" and "Fiddlers' Contest."22

Peter Monro Jack considered Illinois Poems with a number of other recently published volumes of poetry and gave it only two brief paragraphs. He remarked that the book, distinctly unlike the work which first brought Masters fame, was nostalgic, pictorial, and sentimental. It seemed odd to the reviewer that the poet who had done so much to destroy the concept of Friendship Village had now completely reversed himself. Masters in his old age remembered everything pleasantly--the flowers, the trees, the towns, the rivers, and even the people. 23 Ruth Lechlitner was equally succinct in her review. She called Illinois Poems completely indigenous and good regional verse but she failed to find anything distinguished in it. Certain poems which celebrated local landmarks such as "Concord Church" and "Starved Rock" she approved of, and she noted Masters's mixture of nostalgia for the past and distaste for modern industrialism. Like other critics, the reviewer felt that Masters was most at home in free verse and ought to have used that medium more frequently. 24

Along the Illinois concluded Masters's career as a poet who published his verse in book form. Forty-four years had elapsed since the appearance of A Book of Verses in 1898, a period in which Masters had attempted to use every poetic form. Blank verse, free verse, quatrains, rhymed couplets, sonnets, villanelles, limericks flowed from his seemingly inexhaustible pen for almost half a century, and his name was subscribed to dramatic, narrative, lyrical, and descriptive verse dealing with an extraordinary range of subject matter.

Today most of Masters's verse is out of print and there has never been a collected edition of his poetry. Even a paperback edition of his most famous work, Spoon River Anthology, was late in appearing and much of his output is available only in libraries. Only the literary historians seem to be aware of the enormous versatility and productivity of the man, and they have not always been perceptive or

Later Verse

generous in their judgments. The next chapter will suggest how the evaluations of Masters as poet, dramatist, historian, biographer, and novelist--as literary man in general-- have fluctuated. Literary reputations have a habit of dimming and brightening, apparently without real cause. One thinks of John Donne and John Galsworthy, of Herman Melville and F. Scott Fitzgerald, of Herman Hesse and Marcel Proust. At the moment Masters's poetical fame seems to be in heavy eclipse. _Mais qui sait?_ The man's knowledge, courage, industry, candor, energy, and tenacity may well mean more to future readers than the aesthetic aberrations, the crudities and lapses of style, that every perceptive reviewer pointed out.

Notes

1. ELM, _Lichee Nuts_ (New York, 1930), 11, 69, 97.

2. William Rose Benét, "Round About Parnassus," _Saturday Review of Literature_ (October 25, 1930), 7: 270.

3. _New York Times Book Review_ (November 2, 1930), 16.

4. Ruth Lechlitner, "In Mott Street," _New York Herald Tribune Books_ (December 7, 1930), 40. Quotation from _Lichee Nuts_, 75.

5. W. E. Garrison, "Stars, Atoms and Men," _Christian Century_ (December 18, 1935), 52: 1625-1626.

6. Wilbert Snow, "Masters' Reflective Poetry," _New York Herald Tribune Books_ (December 29, 1935), 6.

7. William Rose Benét, "The Phoenix Nest," _Saturday Review of Literature_ (October 19, 1935), 12: 24-25, No. 25.

8. I. F., "Masters, Twenty Years Later," _Christian Science Monitor_ (September 28, 1935), 14.

9. Peter Monro Jack, "The New Books of Poetry," _New York Times Book Review_ (January 12, 1936), 15.

10. Dilys Powell, "New Poetry," _Spectator_ (December 20, 1935), 155: 1040.

11. London Times Literary Supplement (November 23, 1935), No. 1764, 774.

12. Philip Blair Rice, "Late Flowering," Nation (October 16, 1935), 141: 445.

13. "Poets & People," Time (August 31, 1936), 28: 47, No. 9.

14. William Rose Benét, "The Phoenix Nest," Saturday Review of Literature (September 12, 1936), 14: 20, No. 20.

15. Ben Belitt, "Markers for the Dead," Nation (September 26, 1936), 143: 368-370.

16. London Times Literary Supplement (October 24, 1936), No. 1812, 853.

17. Michael Roberts, "Evanescent Blues," Spectator (September 25, 1936), 157: 512.

18. Kerker Quinn, "Heroes for Spoon River," New York Herald Tribune Books (August 30, 1936), 13.

19. Desmond Hawkins, "Recent Verse," Spectator (December 15, 1939), 163: 878.

20. "Simple Folk," London Times Literary Supplement (November 4, 1939), No. 1970, 644.

21. Harry Roskolenko, "Bitter, Lonely, American," Poetry: A Magazine of Verse (January, 1940), 55: 211-214.

22. Coleman Rosenberger, "Two Midwesterners," Poetry: A Magazine of Verse (December, 1941), 59: 164-166.

23. Peter Monro Jack, "The New Books of Poetry," New York Times Book Review (January 4, 1942), 5.

24. Ruth Lechlitner, "From a Prairie Poet," New York Herald Tribune Books (August 10, 1941), 9.

CHAPTER 10

MASTERS IN HISTORY AND ANTHOLOGY

Literary historians have not always been kind to Edgar Lee Masters. The early volumes which won only casual recognition, the phenomenal success of Spoon River Anthology when the poet had reached the age of forty-seven, the long succession of novels, narrative verse, biography, and autobiography which enjoyed only diminishing popularity --all these tended to make the task of the chronicler of American literature highly complex, and they go far to explain the relatively low place to which Masters has been assigned in our national letters. Certainly it is hard to justify the exclusion of Masters from Norman Foerster's widely used and frequently reprinted anthology, American Poetry and Prose (first edition, 1925); or to account for the contempt shown by Roy Harvey Pearce in his Continuity of American Poetry (1961), in which Spoon River Anthology is not even mentioned and there are only two allusions to Masters. Nevertheless, in the last fifty years Masters was considered in various ways by a large group of historians, critics, and anthologists; their verdicts vary considerably and the amount of space allocated to Masters shows surprising fluctuations. A survey of these evaluations will constitute the final chapter of this record of Masters criticism.

The first cooperative history of American literature, jointly edited by William P. Trent, Stuart P. Sherman, John Erskine, and Carl Van Doren, appeared from 1917 to 1921 in what eventually were four volumes entitled The Cambridge History of American Literature. It included essays by various academic figures in addition to the major editors and extensive bibliographical material. As one might expect, Masters received little attention here. Spoon River Anthology was still too new and the free verse movement had not yet received academic blessing. Actually there are only three references to Masters and no discussion of him in the entire work. But it might be added that Herman Melville was also rather summarily treated, reduced to a few pages in a chapter by Van Doren on the minor novelists who were contemporaries of Cooper. The old French proverb to the contrary, times do change.

When the Macmillan Company published the Literary History of the United States in 1948, another cooperative venture edited by Robert E. Spiller, Willard Thorp, Thomas H. Johnson, and Henry Seidel Canby, the entire emphasis in writing American literary history had altered. Literature itself received a much broader interpretation, many of the nineteenth century writers were reevaluated and often downgraded, and recent novelists and poets were given generous space. Willard Thorp included Masters in his survey of the "new" poetry (chapter lxx) and allotted the poet two pages, a little less space than that given to Lindsay or Sandburg. Thorp observed that Masters was aided by his training as a lawyer and by his choice of the epitaph form; he was compelled to look at his material sharply and his literary medium assured brevity. The success of Spoon River Anthology was also in part the result of timeliness. American readers were increasingly aware of stains and blotches on the national facade. In Thorp's words, "Masters' Spoon River was the first village to have its shroud of decency violently removed." The critic ended with the usual judgment that Masters, despite productivity which averaged better than one book a year, never again approached his achievement of 1915.1

Three years later a third cooperative literary history appeared, The Literature of the American People, the joint work of Kenneth B. Murdock, Arthur H. Quinn, Clarence Gohdes, and George F. Whicher. This single volume of 1172 pages included a chapter entitled "Analysts of Decay," in which Masters received three brief paragraphs. Professor Whicher was unsympathetic with contemporary writing (see for example his imperceptive accounts of Hemingway and Faulkner) and found little of consequence to say about Masters. He made a few desultory comments about Spoon River Anthology and remarked that the epitaph form checked the poet's natural tendency toward diffuseness. Masters's later work, he thought, showed "a laborious but uninspired talent." All in all, Masters remains "a conspicuous example of an author who owes his prominence to a single lucky hit, a book of the moment, rather than to his own personal qualities or artistic distinction."2

Single volume histories of American literature which appeared early in the twentieth century naturally paid no attention to Masters, although brief discussions were sometimes incorporated into revised editions. William P. Trent's History of American Literature, published in 1903, obviously omitted Masters, but the second edition of 1919 did also. William B. Cairns of the University of Wisconsin, usually identified as the first American college teacher to hold the title of professor of American literature, had nothing to say about Masters in his History of American Literature in 1912. But when he published an amplified version of his book in 1930 he commented on the possible indebtedness of the Spoon River author to Edwin Arlington Robinson, Harriet Monroe, and W. M. Reedy, and credited Masters with writing concise, well rounded inscriptions which had a wide appeal despite their pessimistic naturalism. Percy H. Boynton in his History of American Literature, published in 1919, called Spoon River Anthology "in all probability the most widely circulated book of new poems in the history of American literature."3 Despite his adherence to the school of Victorian critics with their natural squeamishness about matters of sex, Boynton tried hard to analyze Masters's work objectively. He did not admire the poet's candor or what he called the caustic informality of the sketches, but he praised Masters for his searching analyses of character, especially in the dramatic monologues which reminded him of Browning. Boynton also gave evidence of familiarity with other poems by Masters than the Spoon River epitaphs. He compared the 400-line "To-morrow Is My Birthday" with the similar poem by Robinson, each work imagining a conversation between Shakespeare and Ben Jonson on the eve of the great dramatist's death. Where Robinson was concise about sex matters, Masters was prolix and gross. Boynton admitted, however, that the thrills and shocks which seemed to be promised by Spoon River Anthology did not really materialize in Masters's later work. When Fred Lewis Pattee published his History of American Literature Since 1870 in 1917 he made no reference to Masters. But thirteen years later, in The New American Literature, Pattee devoted several pages to what he called "perhaps the most talked of, perhaps the most influential, book of poems since Leaves of Grass."4 Pattee traced Masters's lineage and commented that the anthology had a certain shock value which accounted for its immediate acceptance. The epitaphs not only dealt candidly with sex but they were also ruthless, even blasphemous. Moreover, the book had little real characterization and little description; it was exposition in story form. Fifteen years after the poems appeared in a volume with Masters identified as the author, Pattee could see that some of the early criticism was ludicrously generous; yet in his considered opinion the Spoon River collection was both original and unique.

As early as the decade of the 1920's Masters began to attract attention among foreign historians of American literature. Régis Michaud devoted space to Masters in his Panorama de la littérature Américaine contemporaine. He identified the Spoon River poet as a rebel who mobilized Olympus against the Puritan Jehovah. Although fundamentally a satirist and a caricaturist, Masters had succeeded in giving human portraits in depth; indeed, he liberated his dead souls through their confessions. The interminable Domesday Book, Michaud remarked, lacked the impact of the anthology but Masters had proved himself to be a painter, a storyteller, a satirist, and a lyricist whose genius took many tones. "Rarement les illusions de l'homme moyen ont été aussi bien et ironiquement célébrées."5 Another brief foreign estimate came from a German critic, Walther Fischer, a professor at the University of Giessen. In his Die Englische Literatur der vereinigten Staaten von Nordamerika Fischer said of the Spoon River people: "es sind 214 knappe Grabinschriften im kurzen, prosaähnlichen Freivers, in denen die Verstorbenen einer typischen westlichen Kleinstadt ihre Lebensschicksale monologisieren." He also added a sentence about the Domesday Book: "Auch seine späteren Werk setzen die Kleinstadtsatire fort."6 Only a few years later the Englishman A. C. Ward published his American Literature 1880-1930. He recognized the significance of Spoon River Anthology but suggested that the book was redundant and needed itself to be anthologized. Masters, he contended, had overdone the misery and wretchedness of the inhabitants of the famous village; fewer studies of morbidity would have made the collection more convincing and impressive. Ward also criticized the roughness of the free verse, although he conceded that Masters's literary form was a pleasant corrective to the excessive smooth rhyming of an earlier decade. In a later chapter Ward considered the biographical writing of the period and commented briefly on Masters's life of Lincoln. He thought the volume deserved no praise at all since the biographer's method was "to sprinkle soot over Lincoln from every angle."7

Later works by transatlantic critics continued to emphasize the originality and durable influence of Masters's work, although they too concentrated on Spoon River Anthology and tended to slight everything else. Léonie Villard, a professor at the University of Lyon who published La poésie Américaine in 1945, discussed Masters in her chapter on the poetic renaissance of 1914. Although her account has some factual errors (she placed Reedy's Mirror in Chicago rather than in St. Louis, and she called Anne Rutledge "le seul personnage historique dans la série purement fictive des habitants de Spoon River"),8 she was enthusiastic about the poet's achievement. She pointed out that the Spoon River dead bared not only their frailties, their errors, and their crimes but their virtues and merits as well. Lucinda Matlock, Anne Rutledge, and Cassius Hueffer were admirable people. Mlle. Villard also emphasized the point that the anthology was indeed a series of memorable portraits but it was also a microcosm: "il recrée pour nous, avec la vie d'une bourgade du Moyen Ouest, certains aspects essentiels de la vie d'un pays et d'un époque."9 In sum Masters had realized the wish of Whitman that the American scene could supply both substance and inspiration to true poets. In an appendix the critic reprinted four Spoon River portraits: Amelia Garrick, Archibald Higbie, Jeremy Carlisle, and Oaks Tutt--none of them, curiously enough, among the best known figures in Masters's portrait gallery.

In 1948 Charles Cestre of the Sorbonne published two books on American writers, one a brief sketch of the literary panorama, the other a more concentrated study of selected nineteenth and twentieth century poets. In La littérature Américaine Cestre identified Masters as a Chicago lawyer who composed malicious portraits in free verse and presented them as cemetery epitaphs. In form they were caricatures, confessions, dialogues, even dramatic actions, all of which exposed hypocrisies and revealed secret motives. Cestre thought that Masters was not always a poet but claimed that he frequently found the exact image or metaphor to convey his meaning effectively.10 In Les poètes Américains Cestre dealt with such disparate poets as Longfellow, Whitman, Robinson, and Frost. He gave Masters a chapter of ten pages. Cestre commented shrewdly that American literary taste had changed sharply since the days when patriotic odes and tributes to national heroes had satisfied readers. Writers now, as Cestre put it, "agitaient le boue" (muck-raked), with complete impunity. Masters himself "révèle les mauvaises pensées restées secrètes, les mauvaises actions restés cachées; ou il exprime les aveux et les

remords."11 The mood of Spoon River was generally pessimistic; religion was only an illusion, politics was corrupt,
happiness was rare. Cestre observed that Masters provided
only profiles, not finished sketches of his characters, but he
cited many memorable examples and printed some of the epitaphs in French translation. In general he thought that
Spoon River Anthology owed its success to qualities such as
humor, sharp observation, concision, and dramatic construction which were commonly ascribed to prose. But although
Masters probably lacked an ear for verbal harmony he could
also write occasional passages of veritable poetry. Certainly he possessed imagination. Like other critics, Cestre
thought badly of Masters's subsequent work. The New
Spoon River was only a pale copy of the original. Domesday Book was a novel in verse without interest. And one of
the last collections, Poems of People, "cherche un effet
nouveau dans l'emploi du langage populaire, sans véritable
gain pour la poésie."12 Cestre was almost the only foreign
critic who showed much familiarity with the collections of
verse that Masters published toward the end of his life.

In the 1950's two Swiss professors of English wrote
histories of American literature. Heinrich Straumann of the
University of Zurich devoted two pages to Masters in his
short chronicle of twentieth century writing and pointed out
that a "strong element of psychological reflection in the
quest for truth on the nature of man" provided the basis for
Spoon River Anthology. 13 Straumann saw that Masters was
fundamentally concerned with the discrepancy between appearance and reality in human life, a conception which accounted for some of the most striking poems in the collection. He called attention to the four portraits of the Pantier
family and to such isolated epitaphs as those of Elijah
Browning and Webster Ford. Henry Lüdeke, of the University of Basel, produced a much more ambitious book, Geschichte der Amerikanischen Literatur, a volume of 653
pages with an extensive bibliography. Lüdeke remarked the
fanfare which greeted Spoon River Anthology but was unimpressed by subsequent work, "als seine voluminöse übrige
Produktion an Gedichten, Dramen, Romanen und sonstiger
Prosa keinen Eindruck machte und heute so gut wie verges-
sen ist."14 In the critic's opinion, Masters was considerably less important than Robert Frost. "Aber Masters' his-
torische Bedeutung als der Herold der neuen Dichtung bleibt
dabei unangetastet."

Cyrille Arnavon of the University of Lyon published

his Histoire littéraire des États-Unis in 1953 and gave Masters a brief but generous evaluation. The tombstone sketches, Arnavon pointed out, "montrent surtout, pour employer le vocabulaire freudien, des refoulés, des névrosés, des schizophrènes"; but the book read like a novel despite the brevity of the epitaphs and their cruel realism. Arnavon also praised the autobiography, Across Spoon River, as the work of a consummate artisan in letters and a skillful technician in verse. Masters saved naturalism from its most frequent artistic weakness, a defect of structure. The French critic had no doubt about the significance of Masters's chief work: "Spoon River durera."15

Another French survey of American literature appeared in 1954. But John Brown's Panorama de la littérature contemporaine aux États-Unis was loosely written and often inaccurate. Brown, an American diplomat with extensive European experience, treated Masters very briefly and called Spoon River Anthology a Winesburg, Ohio in free verse. Both Masters and Sherwood Anderson, he thought, described the same frustrated and tormented souls.

Long before the 1950's, of course, various American critics took the opportunity to evaluate Masters, brief as some of their estimates were. As early as 1918, Van Wyck Brooks, before embarking on his multi-volume study of our native letters, spoke discerningly of Spoon River Anthology in his Letters and Leadership. The book, he thought, had an immense and legitimate vogue. Masters was perhaps exaggerating in picturing the suicidal and murderous tendencies of his villagers, but he was quite correct in revealing the spiritual isolation in which the people lived. Brooks, using words that must have pleased H. L. Mencken, alluded to the prairie community as a cultural desert.16 Only a few years later Carl and Mark Van Doren, in their American and British Literature Since 1890, praised Masters as a satirist and hence a writer to be cherished since satirists were not too common in American literature. Masters condemned cruelty and meanness as vigorously as he praised magnanimity and courage. Being basically a rebel he was not invariably an artist. But he brought to American poetry "one of its most robust intelligences."17

At least half a dozen books appeared in the 1930's which took the occasion to evaluate Masters as a poet and an important American literary figure. Most of the treatments are repetitious, providing the usual minimum of biographical data, praise for Spoon River Anthology, and a cautious estimate of the writer's other achievements. With the exception of Ludwig Lewisohn, the critics expressed serious reservations about Masters's ultimate position.

Russell Blankenship's American Literature, published in 1931 and revised in 1949, placed Masters midway between a cool scientific dissector of character like Robinson and a furious evangelist like Lindsay. Blankenship remarked that if anyone reading Spoon River Anthology for the first time would be impressed by its objectivity, gained by the poet's economy of means. He also called attention to Masters's colloquial and concise language, which nevertheless did not prevent occasional beautiful cadences. Contrary to some opinions, Masters did not attack rusticity per se or draw up a blanket indictment of a small town. Characters like Lucinda Matlock, Doc Hill, and Fiddler Jones were not ridiculed; but Masters did loathe hypocrisy, smugness, and meaningless conformity to convention. Blankenship did not limit his comments to the anthology. He found merit in the New Spoon River and sincerely praised the much-reprinted poem "Silence."[18]

In Expression in America Ludwig Lewisohn grouped Spoon River Anthology with Babbitt and Sister Carrie as works of signal value for future historians of American civilization. He then compared the two anthologies and pointed out that if the 1915 volume was chiefly descriptive and revelatory, the 1924 volume was accusatory. The two works were really a unit marked by a crescendo of intensity. Lewisohn, oddly enough, contended that Masters was one of the few writers of his acquaintance who had style, but he quickly added that by style he meant not gracefulness and manner but rather severity of mind and character. Masters was not a utopian dreamer but a writer who thought accurately and revealed life creatively. If Masters wrote too much and too casually, time could be depended upon to prune and abbreviate his work. But a solid core would always remain.[19]

In his widely read The Great Tradition Granville Hicks had little to say about Masters. Indeed, in his chapter on the poetry of the imagist period he chose to emphasize Amy Lowell, Lindsay, Sandburg, Robinson, and Frost. Discussion of other poets such as Aiken, Pound, and Masters would add little, and therefore he chose to disregard them.[20] Walter Fuller Taylor was moderately enthusiastic in his A History of American Letters and called Spoon River Anthology a modern classic. If many of the monologues dealt with defeated lives, others such as Archibald Higbie and Daisy Fraser were amusing; while the epitaphs of John Cabanis, Anne Rutledge, and Davis and Lucinda Matlock showed courage, vitality, and even a kind of stoicism. Taylor felt that the portraits were only partly realistic and that many were controlled by the author's personal hostility to the materialism and cramped morality of the Middle West.[21] Vernon Loggins, in I Hear America, said bluntly that only one of Masters's thirty-odd volumes was important. He agreed with Charles Cestre that many of the distinctive traits of Spoon River Anthology were those commonly associated with prose but insisted that Masters's work possessed witty epigrams, ironic understatement, and memorable satire. These discrepancies perhaps explained why Masters was often an uneven artist. Loggins also remarked that Masters seemed to find sex and greed the great driving forces of modern life and shaped his literary work in accordance with that concept.[22]

When William Rose Benét solicited works from various American poets to represent them in his Fifty Poets, An American Anthology, Masters replied with his "Seven Cities of America," at the moment unpublished but later collected. He also appended a revealing personal note:

I have no single poem by which I could wish to be remembered. If I have written such a poem I don't know what it is. But for your purpose I am enclosing The Seven Cities of America, not very brief, not yet in any book, but if you want it for your book, go ahead. I think as well of it as anything I have written in a long while. It is a recent composition--last week.[23]

Benét's headnote to the poem was chiefly informative, but the anthologist did remark that Spoon River Anthology was one of the few works of contemporary American literature with some claim to permanence.

Specific histories of American poetry have not been numerous, and those that have appeared have not always been favorable to Masters, though only Roy Harvey Pearce chose virtually to exclude him. In 1929 Alfred Kreymborg published Our Singing Strength, a highly personal account of American verse with some captious judgments. Kreymborg called Masters "perhaps the most tragic figure in modern American poetry," basically "an analytical realist who achieved one great success, but never a single great poem." [24] Kreymborg believed that the "lawyer-poet" simply did not know how to sing. Masters wrote far too much and actually contributed more to American prose than to American poetry. Spoon River Anthology, to be sure, contained a large amount of human material and some remarkable portraits. Masters was also an excellent story teller. But he had an insensitive ear and a questionable sense of beauty. Also, his free verse tended to be heavy-footed. Kreymborg even assailed one of Masters's best known epitaphs, that of Lucinda Matlock, which he called banal. "One admires the old lady and respects her pioneer life, but one simply does not feel it." [25] The critic admitted that Spoon River Anthology was an earnest of things to come, a book to which future poets would undoubtedly be indebted. But the great poet which the anthology implied or perhaps even suggested never materialized. Kreymborg believed that artistically Masters was notably inferior to Carl Sandburg, whom he described in 1914 as "a lanky galoot, with a bang over one eye."

In their History of American Poetry, 1900-1940, published in 1946, Horace Gregory and Marya Zaturenska gave Masters a half dozen pages and quoted the portraits of Thomas Trevelyan and the Village Atheist. The editors called Masters "an archetype of the zealously independent, slowly maturing, Middle Western American of his generation" who read widely if somewhat desultorily, and then, under the influence of Robert Ingersoll and late nineteenth century scientists, developed a ruggedly liberal stance. Their criticism centered on Spoon River Anthology and its sequel, and they concluded that if much of the later work was disappointing, it always had the merits of courage and sincerity. The Domesday Book and The Fate of the Jury, novels in verse rather than poems, were cited as the best known but somewhat disheartening examples of the poet's later style. Once again Masters was considered largely as a one-book man, whom readers could nevertheless respect for his semi-belligerent and independent attitude toward the world. Masters was compared to Theodore Dreiser, both writers being notable for their sturdy but graceless exterior. [26]

Masters received considerable discussion in a more specialized study of American poetry by Frederick William Conner entitled Cosmic Optimism. [27] Conner's approach is more intellectual than artistic; indeed, he makes no value judgments of Masters's poetry at all. He is concerned only with the treatment of evolution in the work of American poets from Emerson to Robinson. It is, of course, well known that Masters read extensively in science and reflected the views of Huxley, Spencer and Darwin in many of his poems. Conner, though, found little development of the theme of evolution in Masters's early books; even Spoon River Anthology reveals scant evidence of the poet's concern with the evolutionary hypothesis. But in such volumes as Songs and Satires and The Great Valley, both published in 1916, Masters began to present evolution with optimistic concern, and in Invisible Landscapes, almost twenty years later, Conner claimed that "he made specific the immaterialist ontology." Such poems as "Neanderthal" and "Ultimate Selection" are particularly clear examples of the poet's acceptance of cosmic optimism. The peculiar nature of Conner's inquiry is quickly apparent when one realizes that not one of the poems selected for discussion by the critic is ever mentioned in an examination of Masters as poet or literary artist. Yet Conner quotes from Masters's autobiography to prove the writer's addiction to science as well as his insistence that a streak of mysticism in his own make-up prevented him from ever becoming a dyed-in-the-wool naturalist.

Masters got considerable attention in Fred B. Millett's Contemporary American Authors, the 1940 edition of which included a critical survey and 219 bio-bibliographies. Millett considered Masters's work in three areas: poetry, biography, and autobiography. His remarks on Spoon River Anthology, which he deemed a "notorious volume," reveal no new approach but vigorous comment. Masters, he thought, had turned life in a small Illinois village inside out for the disapprobation of a horrified world. The tributes carved on tombstones were quite different from the epitaphs spoken by the tormented denizens of the cemetery, and the audacity shown by Masters in his portraits "won the book a scandalous as well as poetic triumph."28 About the poetic value of the book Millett was less certain; the unrhymed verse showed occasional cadences but the diction was commonly below the level of "decorous colloquial language." Yet Masters could at times produce really moving poetry, as the epitaph of Anne Rutledge proved. Masters's subsequent work was unimpressive, the Domesday Book being obviously inferior to Browning and The New Spoon River suffering from the usual disadvantage of a sequel. But Spoon River Anthology, Millett admitted, was "an unforgettable panorama of American life."

In a very different kind of study, namely regional literary history, Masters assumed considerable significance, although the emphasis fell not on aesthetic values but on his representation of a given area and cultural environment or on his influence upon other writers. In a sense Masters was a kind of spokesman for the Middle West more than he was a novelist, dramatist, or poet.

At least four books of this kind merit some attention. The earliest was Harry Hansen's Midwest Portraits of 1923. Hansen himself, born in Davenport in 1884, a graduate of the University of Chicago, and for half a dozen years the literary editor of the Chicago Daily News, was a member of the so-called midwestern school of writers. The men he wrote about he had known personally: Sandburg, Anderson, Herrick, Hecht, and Masters, many of them habitues of Schlogl's famous Chicago tavern and all of them prominent in the Chicago literary landscape. The chapter on Masters is sandwiched between one on Anderson, the "corn-fed mystic," and one on Hecht, "the Pagliacci of the Fire Escape." In a sense Hansen was too close to his subjects to have any objectivity; it was perhaps in realization of this fact that he provided more personal details than critical evaluations of Masters's writing.

Hansen emphasized that Masters had grown up in the Lincoln country and that Spoon River Anthology "portrayed a composite community drawn from his knowledge of the little towns along the Sangamon river."29 Hansen also was aware of Masters's slow literary maturity; the early verse, he pointed out, was dignified and formal, often indeed unoriginal and stilted. But the Illinois environment had an early appeal to the young poet, while adolescent reading in Goethe and Whitman proved to be influential later. Hansen saw merit in The New Spoon River and also observed in Masters something of the prophet or exhorter, since even in the Sangamon Valley one who was sincere in his quest could find great spiritual truths. Hansen also felt that Masters was a keen observer of the progress of the republic, a critic who could perceive political crises or lash the stupidities of legislators. The novel Mitch Miller, he remarked, contained keen comment on national affairs within the framework of a boy's story.

Concerning himself more with literary matters, Hansen claimed that Masters, more than anyone else of the so-called Chicago school, showed extraordinary versatility in both verse and prose. The Domesday Book and Children of

the Market Place were good examples of this ability, while
the recently published Skeeters Kirby afforded strong evidence
of Masters's continued growth and promise. Hansen admitted
that in the years following Spoon River Anthology Masters had
not duplicated his great success, but he exonerated him from
any obligation to do so. For Masters had remarkable gifts
which made him loom large in the Middle Western literature
of the period.

Some twenty years after Hansen's book Bernard Duffey published his The Chicago Renaissance in American Letters, A Critical History.[30] Duffey considered such writers
of the 1890's as Henry B. Fuller and Eugene Field but devoted his principal chapters to Sherwood Anderson and the
Illinois triad of poets, Sandburg, Lindsay, and Masters. The
oldest of the three poets and the first to publish verse, Masters was distinguished as an early figure in the development
of liberal thought. Duffey traced his revolt against small
town conformity and his rather reluctant decision to study
law. To the critic, Masters's early reading of Shelley was
almost as significant as his later exposure to the ideas of
Huxley and Spencer, but probably the real emancipation from
conventionality came in the Chicago years when Masters became the law partner of Clarence Darrow and was early accepted into the somewhat riotous confraternity of the Chicago
Press Club. Duffey was more interested in tracing the development of Masters's liberalism in the Chicago environment
than in assessing his role as a poet, although he did clarify
some of the details about the original composition of Spoon
River Anthology and alluded to the "liberals" in the Illinois
village: Wendell Bloyd, Immanuel Ehrenhardt, Seth Compton,
George Trimble, and John Cabanis--none of them, it might be
noted, among the more famous citizens of the community.
Duffey contended, incidentally, that the Spoon River portraits
owed a good deal to the friendship of Theodore Dreiser and
Carl Sandburg, a point of view without general support. The
Chicago Renaissance in American Letters, despite some careless and inaccurate writing, is a competent account of the
period. Masters emerges from Duffey's evaluation as one of
the intellectual leaders of the movement, if not as a great poet. However, the numerous volumes which succeeded Spoon
River Anthology are all but ignored, although extensive quotations are made from the autobiography, Across Spoon River.

The most substantial volume to deal with the literary
life of the Middle West in the first three decades of the twentieth century was published by Dale Kramer in 1966. Also

entitled Chicago Renaissance, it was based not only on the autobiographical and reminiscent volumes of the chief figures in the movement but also on their correspondence and on interviews with many of the writers themselves. Kramer's approach to his subject was clearly indicated by the title given to the first part of his study. "Six Poor Boys in Search of Themselves." The youths selected were Floyd Dell, Sherwood Anderson, Theodore Dreiser, Carl Sandburg, Vachel Lindsay, and Edgar Lee Masters, none of them, it should be noted, Chicago-born but all of them closely associated for some years with the intellectual life of the Windy City. Kramer dealt with his subjects alternately, tracing their background, education or lack thereof, early literary experience, marital adventures, and ultimate success. His account is certainly the liveliest chronicle of the period so far published, if occasionally wanting in coherence and obviously centered more on personalities than on sober analysis of the various literary works. Kramer's comments on Masters occupy some fifty pages but are scattered throughout the book. In his acknowledgement of sources, incidentally, he claimed that Masters was the most interesting character in his portrait gallery--"perhaps because at first, judged on his published photographs and autobiographical writings, he appeared so monumentally dull."31

Although Kramer did not set out to write a biography of any of his chosen figures he did provide a good many details about each, many of them unfamiliar. Thus he tells more about Masters's boyhood and youth, particularly about his relations with his family and early Chicago friends, than Masters himself revealed in Across Spoon River, the result of conversations with Masters's daughter, his nephew, and one of his secretaries. Equally detailed are the accounts of Masters's marriage to Helen Jenkins, which ended in divorce in 1923, and his relationship with Tennessee Mitchell, later the wife of Sherwood Anderson. One of the best sections of the book is the nineteenth chapter, "Poems Written Half in Jest," in which Kramer managed to recapitulate the familiar story of the composition of Spoon River Anthology with novelty and verve.

Since Chicago provided his chronological and geographical background Kramer did not follow Masters to his somewhat lonely residence at the Hotel Chelsea in New York, nor did he make any comment on the later writings. Indeed, Chicago Renaissance is substantially better as a subjective, even gossipy account of writers striving for a foothold in the social and economic environment of a big city than as an evaluation of their literary work, whether it took the form of poetry or fiction. But certainly Kramer succeeded in defining Masters's personality as few other biographers or critics have.

Michael Yatron's **America's Literary Revolt** is a much narrower book and one with a somewhat doubtful thesis. Yatron was interested chiefly in Populism as it extended into the twentieth century. He claimed that it was both reactionary and xenophobic, particularly hostile to those who did not possess a farm background. The chief literary Populists, in his estimation, were Vachel Lindsay, Carl Sandburg, and Edgar Lee Masters.

Undoubtedly Masters shared some of the Populist views. His background was rural, he was sympathetic with agrarianism, he placed Jefferson at the head of American statesmen and certainly had a nostalgic yearning for a land of small villages and self-dependent farmers, and he was fundamentally opposed to domination by eastern capitalists and industrialists. But the breadth of his intellectual interests and his sophisticated liberalism removed him as far from the Populist camp as his father Hardin Masters was removed from the conservative establishment of the Sangamon Valley. Somehow the label of Populist, even if defined in the broadest terms, does not seem particularly appropriate for Masters.

Yatron, although he drew his evidence from Masters's books, was not deeply concerned with his subject as a man of letters. His literary judgments are casual and superficial. To Yatron, **Spoon River Anthology** was an accident and Masters himself was basically a "prose man" whose craving to achieve eminence as a poet vitiated his prose.32 This negative attitude led Yatron to predict that Masters's verse would not be read in the future but that the writer would have durable importance for the social historian. Readers of Yatron's book should be aware that many proper names are misspelled, titles of poems are often cited inaccurately, and quotations are not always given verbatim.

Before concluding a survey of the literary criticism of Masters's work it might be well to consider how the writer has fared with the anthologists of American literature, the editors of collections intended both for the general reader and for the classroom. Here there is both negative and positive evidence; some widely used anthologies have omitted Masters altogether, some have represented him only by a handful of Spoon River portraits, and others have included an extensive amount of his verse. Anthologists, it should be noted, tend to follow the beaten track. Certainly the epitaphs of Lucinda Matlock, Anne Rutledge, and Petit, the Poet are the hardy perennials of the Masters garden so far as the editors of American literary collections are concerned.

Norman Foerster's failure to include anything by Masters in his highly regarded American Poetry and Prose has already been observed. Masters was also excluded by John Herbert Nelson and Oscar Cargill in their Contemporary Trends, American Literature Since 1900 (1933, revised edition 1949); by Mark Van Doren in his American Poets 1630-1930 (1932); by Jay B. Hubbell in his American Life in Literature (1936); by James D. Hart and Clarence Gohdes in their America's Literature (1955); and by Gay Wilson Allen, Walter B. Rideout, and James K. Robinson in their American Poetry (1965). Since Masters has never achieved the status of a leading figure in American letters he was also obviously omitted from Howard Mumford Jones's and Ernest Leisy's Major American Writers of 1945.

On the other hand, a number of anthologists have included Masters among the authors they selected and have given him ample representation. Perhaps the earliest substantial recognition that Masters received from anthologists came from Harriet Monroe and Alice Corbin Henderson in their The New Poetry, An Anthology (1917). The two editors, associated in Poetry: A Magazine of Verse, chose to reprint "The Hill" and the poem "Silence" plus some nineteen Spoon River portraits (Ollie McGee, Daisy Fraser, Hare Drummer, Doc Hill, Fiddler Jones, Thomas Rhodes, Editor Whedon, Seth Compton, Henry C. Calhoun, Perry Zoll, Archibald Higbie, Father Malloy, Lucinda Matlock, Arlo Will, Aaron Hatfield, H. Herndon, Rutherford McDowell, Anne Rutledge, William and Webster Ford). The selection was judicious, both the misfits or failures and the idealists or enlightened souls being given adequate space. In a new edition of the anthology published in 1932 with biographical and critical notes, "The Hill" and eighteen of the epitaphs were retained but several poems from other volumes by Masters were added: "The Garden," "Desolate Scythia," "My Light with Yours," "Slip-Shoe Lovey," "Christmas at Indian Point," and "The Lake Boats." The editors quite obviously thought that Masters's descriptive and narrative poems often made as much of an impact as the acerbic Spoon River characterizations.

Few subsequent anthologies treated Masters so generously, although he did not want for representation, especially in books of substantial size. Louis Untermeyer in his Modern American Poetry of 1919 found room only for "Silence" and two Spoon River sketches, Lucinda Matlock and Anne Rutledge. In his revised edition of 1921 Untermeyer added "Petit, the Poet" and in a lengthy headnote expressed his admiration for both "Silence" and "Front the Ages With a Smile." The fourth revised edition of this much used book, published in 1930, showed no change. But the combined and enlarged edition of Modern American Poetry and Modern British Poetry which Untermeyer published in 1962 expanded the space accorded Masters. Untermeyer retained "Silence" and the three sketches from the anthology but added "Weekend by the Sea" and "Widows" from Poems of People. He did not alter his earlier critical judgments save to remark that the novels, like some of the later verse, were uneven and that Godbey consisted of thousands of "pedestrian couplets given over to debate and diatribe." But Untermeyer still insisted that the original Spoon River Anthology remained as a milestone.

Conrad Aiken in his Modern Library American Poets 1671-1928 included four Masters poems without editorial comment. But Aiken showed some independence of judgment in this 1929 volume by including not only the familiar "Petit, the Poet" but also the less widely known portraits of Thomas Trevelyan, Edmund Pollard, and Bert Kessler. In 1941 William Rose Benét and Norman Holmes Pearson devoted considerable space to Masters in their Oxford Anthology of American Literature. They selected not only "The Hill," "Johnny Appleseed," and "Beethoven's Ninth Symphony and the King Cobra" but no less than sixteen portraits from the two Spoon River collections (Lucinda Matlock, Thomas Trevelyan, Fiddler Jones, Benjamin Pantier and his wife, Reuben Pantier, Emily Sparks, Daisy Fraser, Anne Rutledge, Trainor the Druggist, The Village Atheist, William and Emily, Robert Chain, Frances Cordell, Richard Harned, and Henry Zoll the Miller). John T. Frederick also included "The Hill" in his regional anthology of 1944, Out of the Midwest; and John T. Flanagan found room for "Lucinda Matlock" and "Fiddler Jones" in America Is West (1945).

F. O. Matthiessen, who compiled the Oxford Book of American Verse in 1950, was probably one of the last anthologists to give Masters extensive space. In his volume of 1132 pages he reprinted "The Hill" and fifteen Spoon River portraits (Cassius Hueffer, Knowlt Hoheimer, Fiddler Jones, Petit the Poet, Elsa Wertman, Hamilton Greene, Editor Whedon, Elliott Hawkins, English Thornton, Jonathan Hough- ton, Father Malloy, Anne Rutledge, Rutherford McDowell, Lucinda Matlock, and Herman Altman). Matthiessen clearly did not limit himself to the sketches previously favored by other anthologists.

In 1955 Clifton Fadiman, in editing The American Treasury 1455-1955, drew material from seven Spoon River epitaphs (John Hancock Otis, The Village Atheist, Seth Comp- ton, Schofield Huxley, Petit, the Poet, Lucinda Matlock, and Anne Rutledge) but did not quote any of them entire and ar- ranged his excerpts under topical headings. W. H. Auden, in choosing material for his Criterion Book of Modern Amer- ican Verse of 1956, selected the sketches of John Horace Bur- leson, Editor Whedon, Perry Zoll, and J. Milton Miles--the last the surprisingly neglected portrait of a man who listened to all the church bells of Spoon River and was unable to de- tect the true from the false.

In 1965 William T. Stafford edited his Twentieth Cen- tury American Writing and reprinted not only "The Hill" but ten portraits from Spoon River Anthology (Cassius Hueffer, Knowlt Hoheimer, Lydia Puckett, Margaret Fuller Slack, Edi- tor Whedon, Daisy Fraser, Mrs. Kessler, Harry Wilmans, Godwin James, and Lucinda Matlock). Stafford also selected two unfamiliar Spoon River sketches, that of Harry Wilmans, who idealistically volunteered to serve in the Spanish-Amer- ican War and died in the Philippines and that of Godwin James, who died equally ignominiously while following the flag of the Kingdom of Heaven.

Not all the anthologists incidentally were American, and not all the anthologies appeared in English. As early as 1928 Eugene Jolas published his Anthologie de la nouvelle poésie Américaine in Paris and included a French translation entitled "Petit, Poète." Jolas also supplied a note about the author:

Son livre Spoon River Anthology, paru il y a une dizaine d'années, a fait une veritable impression par ses qualités de pénétration et d'observation humaines, qui s'attaquèrent surtout, et l'on peut dire pour la première fois en poésie, au puritan- isme du village américain.33

In 1952 Agustí Bartra edited his Antología de la poesia Norte- americana in Mexico City, devoted five pages to Masters, and published Spanish translations of "The Hill" ("La Colina"), five Spoon River sketches (Chandler Nicholas, Anne Rutledge, Petit, El Poeta, Elsa Wertman, and Hamilton Greene), and "My Light With Yours" ("Mi Luz con La Tuya").

Two very recent anthologies of American literature by well known critics suggest that Masters remains a significant figure with some claims to permanence. Cleanth Brooks, Robert Penn Warren, and R. W. B. Lewis in their American Literature, the Makers and the Making (1972) included three poems by Masters ("Knowlt Hoheimer," "Petit, the Poet," and "Rutherford McDowell"), the same number selected from Sandburg and from Lindsay. And Richard Ellmann and Robert O'Clair in their Norton Anthology of Modern Poetry (1973), a volume of some 1400 pages, chose to include fourteen Masters poems ("The Hill," ten portraits from Spoon River Anthology--Cassius Hueffer, Amanda Barker, Frank Drummer, Fiddler Jones, Petit, the Poet, Elsa Wertman, Hamilton Greene, Editor Whedon, Anne Rutledge and Lucinda Matlock--and three portraits from the sequel--Marx the Sign Painter, Rhoda Pitkin, and Unknown Soldiers).

This list of anthologies is by no means exhaustive, but enough collections have been cited to indicate that Edgar Lee Masters remains significant to most of the professional students of American literature. Neither literary historians nor anthologists, to be sure, have any special claims to clairvoyance, nor do their judgments necessarily indicate a consensus. But fifty years after the publication of one of the most widely discussed and one of the most generally read books in American literary history, Masters retains an audience. His artistic limitations no longer excite much discussion, and the reading public seems content to ignore most of his enormous output of verse and prose. But the Spoon River poems and even a handful of his other works are unlikely to die from complete neglect. Indeed a few straws in the wind might even predict a mild revival of interest in a man who was for several decades an important figure in the American literary scene--witness the centennial exhibit and catalogue of his works at the University of Texas, the publication in paperback form of the two anthologies, and the recent revival of the dramatic revision of the Spoon River portraits on the New York stage. Edgar Lee Masters was never one to ignore the ironies of life. It might have pleased his complex soul to know that his portrait would one day adorn a United States postage stamp, even though the six-cent value would be insufficient for an ordinary letter.

Notes

1. Willard Thorp, in Literary History of the United States (New York, 1948), II, 1181. The third volume of this work is devoted exclusively to bibliography; a complete list of Masters's works and a selected list of relevant criticism appear on pp. 638-640.

2. George F. Whicher, in Literary History of the American People (New York, 1951), 870.

3. Percy H. Boynton, A History of American Literature (Boston, 1919), 470.

4. Fred Lewis Pattee, The New American Literature (New York & London, 1930), 285.

5. Régis Michaud, Panorama de la littérature Américaine contemporaine (Paris, 1926), 188-189.

6. Walther Fischer, Die Englische Literatur der vereinigten Staaten von Nordamerika (Wild-Park-Potsdam, 1929), 94.

7. A. C. Ward, American Literature 1880-1930 (New York, 1932), 166-168, 251.

8. Léonie Villard, La poésie Américaine (Paris, 1945), 98-101.

9. Ibid., 104.

10. Charles Cestre, 203.

11. Charles Cestre, Les poètes Américains (Paris, 1948), 105, 106.

12. Ibid., 114.

13. Heinrich Straumann, American Literature in the Twentieth Century (London, 1951), 137.

14. Henry Lüdeke, Geschichte der Amerikanischen Literatur (Bern, 1952), 534.

15. Cyrille Arnavon, Histoire littéraire des États-Unis (Paris, 1953), 361.

16. Van Wyck Brooks, Letters and Leadership (New York, 1918), 15-16.

17. Carl and Mark Van Doren, American and British Literature Since 1890 (New York & London, 1925), 30.

18. Russell Blankenship, American Literature (New York, 1931), 600-605.

19. Ludwig Lewisohn, Expression in America (London, n.d., [1932]), 493.

20. Granville Hicks, The Great Tradition (New York, 1933), 247.

21. Walter Fuller Taylor, A History of American Letters (New York, 1936), 400-402. A useful bibliography of Masters by Harry Hartwick is appended to Taylor's book, pp. 584-585.

22. Vernon Loggins, I Hear America ... Literature in the United States Since 1900 (New York, 1937), 147-151.

23. William Rose Benét, Fifty Poets, An American Auto-Anthology (New York, 1933), 20.

24. Alfred Kreymborg, Our Singing Strength (New York, 1929), later published as A History of American Poetry (New York, 1934), 379.

25. Ibid., 383.

26. Horace Gregory and Marya Zaturenska, A History of American Poetry 1900-1940 (New York, 1946), 227.

27. Frederick William Conner, Cosmic Optimism (Philadelphia, 1949), 351-357, especially p. 353.

28. Fred B. Millett, Contemporary American Authors (New York, 1940), 138. See also pp. 171-172 and 178, where Millett praises the life of Vachel Lindsay as one of the best biographies of an important contemporary poet and Across Spoon River as "a remarkable self-portrait."

29. Harry Hansen, Midwest Portraits (New York, 1923), 244.

30. Bernard Duffey, The Chicago Renaissance in American Letters, A Critical History (n. p. [East Lansing], 1954).

31. Dale Kramer, Chicago Renaissance (New York, 1966), 358-359.

32. Michael Yatron, America's Literary Revolt (New York, 1959), 68-69.

33. Eugene Jolas, Anthologie de la nouvelle poésie Américaine (Paris, 1928), 156-157.

INDEX

Index

Index

Index